NIGHT MOVES

Night Moves

Jessica Hopper

UNIVERSITY OF TEXAS PRESS ❧ AUSTIN

Requests for permission to reproduce material from this
work should be sent to:
Permissions
University of Texas Press
P.O. Box 7819
Austin, TX 78713-7819
utpress.utexas.edu/rp-form

∞ The paper used in this book meets the minimum requirements
of ANSI/NISO Z39.48-1992 (R1997) (Permanence of Paper).

Names: Hopper, Jessica, author.
Title: Night moves / Jessica Hopper.
Description: First edition. | Austin : University of Texas Press, 2018.
Identifiers: LCCN 2018008601 | ISBN 978-1-4773-1788-4 (pbk. : alk.
paper) | ISBN 978-1-4773-1794-5 (library e-book) | ISBN 978-1-4773-
1795-2 (nonlibrary e-book)
Subjects: LCSH: Hopper, Jessica. | Music critics—United States—
Biography. | Music journalists—United States—Anecdotes.
Classification: LCC ML423.H756 A3 2018 | DDC 818/.603 [B]—dc23
LC record available at https://lccn.loc.gov/2018008601

doi:10.7560/317884

*To JR, for teaching me about Chicago
and being down for whatever*

Ain't it funny how the night moves
When you just don't seem to have as much to lose

BOB SEGER, "NIGHT MOVES"

CONTENTS

NORTH AVE

CROTCH

28 2

30

27

24

15

4

6

11

5

MILWAUKEE AVE

16

29

DIVISION ST

20 10

17

22

25

18

AUGUSTA BLVD

14

CHICAGO AVE

26

WESTERN

19 13

3

23

DAMEN AVE

7

WOOD ST

ASHLAND AVE

12 8

9

INDUSTRIAL CORRIDOR

GRAND AVE

1

TRAIN BRIDGE

LAKE ST

21

1 Old Loft*
2 Kinko's
3 Edmar Polish Grocery*
4 Myopic Books
5 Reckless Records*
6 Buddy/heaven lofts*
7 Neighboring punk houses where I lived*
8 Guy peeing on roof
9 Frankie Beverly Car Wash
10 Liquor store
11 Place I thought I'd die
12 Empty school lot next door
13 Ukrainian grind bar
14 Orthodox church
15 Earwax*
16 Where Al left the house naked*
17 Old man Polish bar
18 Empty Bottle
19 Chicago Ave. library
20 Picante
21 Redevelopment condos
22 Rainbo
23 Dollar store
24 Car crash
25 1st Chi. apt.
26 Mecca Fashions*
27 Yuppie jizz disco
28 Quimby's
29 Former home of Nelson Algren
30 Underdog*

*no longer exists

INTRODUCTION

I came back to the Midwest from LA because the penetrability of Southern California light had gotten to me. It was February 1997; I was twenty-one. The days documented in this book begin in spring 2004, a few years into what has since become a two-decade run in Chicago. This book is a testimony, of sorts, to my obsession with the city.

In the early aughts, living in a series of extremely cheap and decrepit apartments on the edge of an industrial corridor, I was an unwitting participant in a wave of gentrification that has since subsumed the area. All the empty lots mentioned here are now condos; the moused-up punk houses were razed for redevelopment and now exist only in collective memory. I was not yet a professional writer but mapped that dream often.

I was hardly ever without my friends. This is as much about their lives in that particular time and space as it is my own.

friends, bikes,
        the long night

THE NIGHT

We met up on bikes while the sun was going down. We were early for the bad movie, so we slurped shakes in the BK parking lot across the street 'til it was time. The movie was terrible—great, lobotomizing fun. Back on the bike. The boys went home, I went to Kinko's and saw my bandmate Al, who had sweated through his shirt with coffee-fueled anxiety, as usual. I went over to JR's for a lemonade, stole two cigarettes, borrowed a Gil Scott-Heron record, we left. Back on the bike.

I held JR's bike while he went into the liquor store. Kids who really were just kids, rolling en masse (a Denali, a Celica, a tricked-out Cutlass) hung in the parking lot and greeted one another with a fluid and immaculate shake—butterfly hands that surrendered into a chest pound below the chains. A gentrified local exited the store and wiped out flat on his back in a puddle, soiling his pleat-fronts and splintering his twelve-pack of Lite. Everyone laughed, including me.

Back on the bike. Out in the city, everyone was on a date, and all the dates were going to parties on bikes, on polished toes peeking from sandal heels. All the girls with bare shoulders. It must be a great thing to love those girls.

July 17, 2004

STICK HUNT

I had an art project on my mind and needed to go find a particular little branch for it. JR came with. We went up to the train/land bridge, despite it being frosty out. Someone had dragged a living room set up here and arranged it across from a makeshift tent house that had blown down long ago. The bottom five windows of the building behind it is my old loft. I knew it had been rehabbed, but I was galled when I noticed the windows. My former spot was 4,400 square feet and only had two windows that opened. The rest were Plexiglas or plywood, nailed shut. I felt resentful. JR noted, "It looks like a hotel now."

JR is a good friend; I explained to him my very long dream from last night that involved doing a Japanese tour as the extra guitarist in a reunited Babes in Toyland. He helped me try to divine a meaning. He did not laugh too hard at me when we arrived back home and I crossed "find stick" off my to-do list.

I like the train bridge because it's so Chicago: ¼ nature, ¼ trash, ¼ industrial, ¼ gleaming rehab condos everywhere you look. You can't beat that view of downtown. Chicago is *so Chicago*—it's like getting mashed in the face with a volume of Sandburg poems.

One day, a few summers ago, a friend and I stood in the same spot whipping rocks, trying to knock out the remaining glass in the panes of an old abandoned meatpacking warehouse. We said we wouldn't leave until we knocked out some of the white panes. After about thirty minutes we realized they were plastic, not painted glass, and couldn't be broken no matter what we threw at them.

January 09, 2007

WANNA SEE SOME MEATY-A-ROIDS?!

The brightest meteor shower in our lifetimes brought us up the North Shore to a park in Glencoe, the darkest place I could ever remember being outdoors. We scanned the sky and lay on a picnic table and cursed the trees that blocked our view and then headed down to the beach. There was a 100,000-watt light shining on the boat slips that was light-polluting our good time, but we waded through the surf to a dark spot behind the parks building, just up the sand a bit. We soon found we were not the only ones with this good idea: a trio of teenage boys with a pocket bong had also claimed this spot.

They could not see we were women double their age.

"So, do you guys go to school or do you work?"

Actually, we're grown-ups.

"Well, I live like a grown-up . . . I'm a gemologist. A graduated gemologist. You know much about diamonds?"

He may have said more, but we were seizing with laughter. They were not fazed; they also bragged to us about both the impressive size and girth of their *at-home* bongs.

We lay there until very very late, and could only see maybe fifteen asteroids dissolving in the atmosphere, not at all like the "up to twelve a minute" that the Internet had claimed. That lying planetarium! It was worth it, so very worth it.

August 13, 2007

JOY OF (WO)MAN'S DESIRING

JR and I were talking social as if we had not already hung out for hours the previous day and caught up on all existing topics. He was at work at the bookstore and took a smoke break; I breaked with him and did the smoking for him. Outside it was eighty and almost 10 p.m. and everyone young was skateboarding and biking and tube-topping and staring each other out, a loose mob up and down the sidewalks to the bike-in movies and bars and nouveau emo discos: all that Wicker Park proffers. We were talking about exercise, to be exact, when a girl lurched forward and excitedly announced it was her birthday. *"Thirtyyy-twooo,"* came out of her mouth in a drunken slurp. "I am going to come in soon and buy all the books I want." She named some authors I didn't know. Her boyf, maybe twenty-four and anemic-looking, poofed in from the ether. As she wreathed her arms around him, he added, "And P. G. Wodehouse, too!" Who'da thunk it, the pale kid with the crustache is a Jeeves enthusiast.

Also tonight was the poetry slam of the at-risk youth, mostly teen moms whose writing was about being sad but sturdy under the weight of motherhood. They read with babies on jutted hips or toddlers bing-bonging teeny heads into the back of their legs. After that there was a DJ, and for a quick fifteen minutes before everyone had to bus back, the girls danced and the toddlers waddled. And then as the sub-bass intro for "It's Going Down" went *bum . . . bum bum*, on the three, I saw a girl back it up and drop while front-strapped with a babe in her BabyBjörn. She moved smooth like she was floating, with one hand supporting her baby's head as she dipped towards the floor. It was reverent and defiant at once; it was a beautiful thing to see.

May 10, 2007

THE PLAGUE OF WHY?

Before JR and I went on our walk today, we were standing in the kitchen talking to Matt, and JR says, "What's that guy doing on the roof?" We turned around and looked at the roof that is directly parallel to our kitchen window and there was a guy down on one knee, with the other leg outstretched, his back to us, his hands in front of him, situated around this pipe opening, like a duct, coming up from the roof. Matt supposed he was fixing the vent and JR and I insisted, "NO HE IS NOT! HE IS PEEING! HE IS PEEING INTO THAT HOUSE!" And we were right! The urinator saw us, looked ashamed, kept pissing, then shook, zipped up, and stood. Then he walked towards the other end of the roof like he was inspecting it or something, all, "La la la just making the rounds . . ." and then went back down the ladder.

I thought of the Robert Capa quote I read last night, about how every picture should ask a question. If there had been a picture of that man tinkling into the duct, it would ask many questions. For example:

1. *Why* is he peeing into the duct?
2. Is that *his* house?
3. Does he know where that duct goes?
4. Is it some weird fetish he has?
5. Does his ex-wife live there with her new boyfriend?
6. Is he a handyman who hates his job?
7. Is our duct next?

I spent the beginning of our walk wondering all this out loud and then Matt and I wondered about it again later. Do I post a missed connection on Craigslist, warning my neighbors that there is a mustachioed mystery urinator roaming our rooftops? It is a grade-A baffler.

January 03, 2007

BORN (AGAIN) IN THE USA

We were walking down Western for a long few blocks, and right before we passed the saint candle memorial in a box, with its xeroxed color RIPs and a thin plywood cross where a man was killed (where JR saw the man die), we began talking of rebirth. Of personal rebirth and of spirit renewed, of life, but how to live it?

About how when you realize that we are perpetually moving closer to death, that when it looms large as life, you get free from a lot of the in-between and unreasonable musts. JR saw a man whose body and spirit had just separated, taken in an instant from being of this world to out of it. He said perspective came quick, one night, maybe two. You make peace with death's swift manners and it raises you up.

I did not remember until I was home, I had had this same revelation—maybe seven years ago—on the same strip of Western Avenue. My life at the time was just smoke, ash. I was all kinds of frightened, but by accident had started believing in god, and started praying hours a day. The revelations of spirit were constant. I made peace with death just south of the Western/North intersection as I was walking alone from the train after a show late one night. A man had been following me slowly in his car for blocks and I tried picking apart whatever I could to be less scared. I got okay with dying in the span of about one hundred feet, in the middle of a plaintive, panicky dialogue with god. It was not so much through force of will as it was just a sense that came upon me. Respect for death's omnipresence.

This weekend we went to Tim's dad's memorial service, at his father's local. The old people at the service, of course, know how to grieve and what to say, how to say it, to hug and not pat the arm awkwardly, and that you bring a hot dish. I watched these older folks, pinochle partners of the past, widower golf buddies, old Mooses with lodge livers; there was nothing unknown in their mourning. It was sure, they knew its form and shape. Our table of kid-friends, we were all moving like nervous atoms because of what we do not know yet.

January 09, 2006

CAN'T BE STOPPED

The best part of the emergency room was my radiologist, who was so earnestly strange that it made me feel like I was in a Lynchian dream sequence. He had a limp, said everything twice like a bad song ("Donotmove./Do. Not. Move."), wore a lab coat with his name on it, and made jokes I did not understand as jokes. He presided over nine neck X-rays, then disappeared for a while. I lay there, staring into the machine above me, which was like a big Cuisinart with a light on the bottom. He came back and said, "We must do it again. In the processor, three of your X-rays landed on top of one another. All together. Like the Three Little Bears." He adjusted the light and leaned in to adjust me. "I figured out who the villain is in that story. Little Red Riding Hood. She ate all their porridge."

He leaned over me again to adjust the light, and I thought, the only time anyone gets this close to my face, it's because they are going to kiss me.

I countered, through my concussed fog, "Little Red Riding Hood is the protagonist, not the villain." Then I passed out.

I got in a car accident. A man in a gray Caprice Classic hit me head-on while he was pulling some extreme traffic move on Western. The worst part—really, the worst, worse than my car being totalled—is that when it happened, I was on the phone with my Nana. My eighty-six-year-old Nana, telling her I was coming to visit soon. And then I was screaming and apologizing and had to hang up on her because there was an exploded airbag, and my car was filling with smoke. I hung up on her, stepped outside the car, and passed out on the blacktop, in traffic. A guy who was spare changing came to my aid and got me to the curb.

Then there were the police and the police made me go in the ambulance. I called Miles and JR and Matt and told them where the ambulance was going and why. And then I was on the gurney and they put a catheter in the back of my hand and things on my fingers and a thing around my neck that made a Velcro sound and strapped me down. I fell asleep, but I woke up when we were going into the ER, rolling rolling under the lights, and I thought of Bushwick Bill on the cover of the Geto Boys' *We Can't Be Stopped* and I wished I had my camera, to preserve this moment for my eventual solo album.

Then I woke up and Miles and JR were standing there leaning over me saying, "Hi, buddy," and the look on JR's face almost made me cry. I explained that I was all strapped down and given the special collar until I was done with all the X-rays and the CT scan to make sure, but that the doctors think I am fine. Just a concussion and smoke inhalation and whiplash. Matt was ready to fly home from tour if anything was wrong, if they were going to keep me at the hospital. "I am fine," I said. "I just wanna get home so I can see Spoon on Letterman," I said. I am tough, but it sure is nice to have such good friends to come pet your hand when you're hurt.

Never been in an ambulance before. The CAT scan was like an oscillating donut. Had also never done that before. I was lying there, forever, after the X-rays and scans, and I was watching my vitals on the monitor behind my head. Every time Miles mentioned the unused "urine bag" stationed next to him, my heart rate went up. We played a little game to see how high we could spike my heart rate: 127 on "urine bag" alone.

September 01, 2005

I'M IN UR PARALLEL UNIVERZ, RIDIN' UR ARMORED ICE BEARZ!

Last weekend, I went to Derek Erdman's birthday party. There was no cake, and he spent the entire time making grilled cheeses so as not to have to deal with anyone. These two teenage girls showed up and were standing in a huddle in a corner. I decided to befriend them and introduce them to people I knew. When I was sixteen and hitting up the parties of the people I worked with at the record store, grown-ups all, I would wind up standing in a corner with my best friend trying to project *Wow I'm having so much fun drinking this beer*, while slugging back the Michelob Light we'd pilfered from her parents' basement fridge. And even though it was totally the lamest lame that ever lamed, we would front to our school friends about the rad party we partied at, and never acknowledge to one another the soul-crushing awkwardness of being the only teenagers at a grown-ups' party.

Derek's birthday day was not a grim experience.

Amy's dog Camille was there, eating edamame.

The girls were asking me and Lil' Dave for recommendations on records they should pick up. "Well, what sort of things do you like?" we asked. They really love Delta 5, and are in a Delta 5 cover band, just the two of them, but it's just French horn and tambourine. We were kind of stunned and professed that they were the coolest people at the party and totally didn't need our help. They pressed on. Dave told them why *Double Nickels* was crucial. I suggested Au Pairs, Slits, that Belgian band Antena, and Disc One of *Best of The Whispers*.

I wanted to ask if I could join their band, but, admittedly, grown-ups can be a corrupting force, and I am already in a new band. Perhaps my band with Kate and JR—Juan of Arc—can play with their eleventh grade chamber-minimalist tribute to Delta 5. TBA!

December 14, 2007

LIFE AFTER GRILLQUITOS

I do not want Christmas break to be over. I still have not finished addressing the New Year's cards I made on 12/14. I read that in France people exchange cards for the holidays well into January. As an expression of my desire for a more French system—primarily socialized medicine—I am sending my cards the French way.

Plus, the kitchen is still not clean. I got it almost all the way clean after the New Year's Eve meal for ten. I cooked saffron rice, butter beans with mint, gingerbread cake with poached apricots in a vanilla reduction, a salad with oranges and fennel in rose water, naan, and vegetarian corn dogs with "special sauce." Miles brought a butternut squash and Gruyère casserole, Ben made green beans. It was too much and so I had more people over for dinner last night, otherwise I'd be eating this rice every day until Arbor Day. Now everything is dirty again, but I can't stop reading long enough to get handy with the mop.

The NYE meal was lovely and candlelit; everyone in attendance was in a mood, either half-sick, utterly allergic, stressing, spiritually fatigued, hungover and near barfing, awkwardly unacquainted with others, or internally miserable over non-dinner-related happenings. Megan came over today and she said the benefit was that everyone seemed to be having a time of it, so at least no one was left out. It was a fellowship of the weirded-out.

After dinner, the plan was we were to burn lists, in the empty lot next door, of what we wanted to leave behind in 2007. I had asked people to bring their lists prepared, but only Megan did. So as a result, everyone sat down with their after-dinner coffee and pondered on all of the bad shit, unwanted feelings, and parts of an ugly past that lingered in their present. Lists were scribbled, boots tugged back on, and out we went.

We put our lists in the jar and Matt rolled his like a wick. The wind kept blowing the lighter out. The notes were folded too tight to light. Matt's note smoldered. It snowed hard and the wind blew and, meanwhile, the physics of burning stuff in a jar was against us. We went through a whole pack of matches. Everyone got nervous and joked about the bad omen. Ben suggested we take them inside and burn them in the bathtub, but by the time we got up there, the jar was smoking full of smoldering notes and so I held it out the bathroom window while we tried to decide what would become of the notes in their fiery state. It smelled terrible so we elected to drown them. Instead, I accidentally turned the shower on myself. The house stank like a campfire. The notes met a watery grave and are resting in peace, dissolving in the mason jar on the back porch. Next year, I insisted, we will drink them.

January 03, 2008

PEOPLE WHO DIED, DIED

We went to Ben and Logan's dance night at the neighborhood bar but did not dance. We watched young
Ukrainian professional girls do a clumsy frontal grind,
their lifted arms lifting their office dresses, and the
guys wearing brown leather coats on the dance floor's
sidelines pointed at the crazy girls with whatever fingers weren't being used to hold their plastic beer cups.
Someone barfed in or around a trash can up front, so
we sat in the back, and I wound up in the same booth
on the same side that somehow I always get stuck in,
the one with the perfect side view of the men's room
urinal. And Miles wonders why I don't go out.

It's the middle-to-ass end of the worst part of the winter. The part where you kind of just give up.

Everyone is smoking again, coasting in and out of a
grim yet unremarkable malaise, sleeping too much or
hardly at all, eating easy heat 'n' serve meals and food
from boxes, trying to get it together enough to make
it to the mailbox and return those Netflixes. We drag

ourselves out of the house to whatever high-fiving party place is on offer and comraderize, talk about how we miss our bikes, and discuss if the Jim Carroll Band has more than one good song, like it matters.

Right before the Peaches song came on, I was telling Kate and Ben about seeing the band Singer the night before. Singer is the Velvet Revolver of the Drag City/ Chicago avant-weird gamut, all-star but not. I liked them best when I did not look at them; they had some good songs with harsh notes. It is as if Rob and the old U.S. Maple guy (Todd? Al? I dunno) are trying to outdo each other with theatrical, concerned concentration and ironic "performer" moves. The appearance is that of a sort of personality-transfer frontline, mewling together, imitating each other. There was a lot of touching of the face going on. Like, tons.

Is holding the mic and posing like you are full throttle in the middle of an aria, but not actually singing a note, a comment on spectacle? Is recoiling from the guitar neck like it has hurt you a statement about the power of music? How about fluttering your hand in front of your face like you are doing a Spanish fan dance? Are they performing about performance with sincerity? Are they just hams? It is hard to tell.

Before they were playing I was telling my friend about the chapter of the book I am working on. He leaned over as the U.S. Maple man was in the middle of me-owing "STAAAAAGECOACH!" and the friend sug-gested including a sidebar about how you shouldn't ever write lyrics that you would be embarrassed to say out loud to your friend. I don't agree entirely, but he's not wrong. As I was telling Ben and Kate this, Peaches started rapping that "I want to see your pussy" song, as if to prove the point. Though, I guess it just depends on what type of friendship you have with someone.

February 06, 2008

PONY HAIR SANDALS

There is nothing quite like a humbling little walk through your hood in your pajamas in the blazing hotness of 8:47 a.m. on a workday. I had not yet brushed my teeth and had been awake maybe fifteen minutes. I was wearing indoor clothes outdoors and the too-big pony hair sandals Heather left on the back porch, which was fortunate because JR's house is kind of far to go sans shoes entirely. Good morning, people with your dogs and fitness routine and your commuter bikes. Good morning, neighbors! Hello, elderly couple that looks scared for me, I am merely locked out. Hello, denizens of Ukrainian Village, I am on my way to the set of spare keys held by my best friend.

After Chicago Avenue, I realized the too-big pony hair sandals were an impediment and if I was looking like such crunkled shit already, what difference did shoes make? I took them off and picked them up in front of the golden Orthodox church while a pacing teenage boy watched. I put the shoes back on to cross Augusta, and then again when I reached the side of the Empty

Bottle, as there were so many lipstick-slicked filters on the ground and the sidewalk is much darker. No one should go barefoot on Western Avenue.

I removed the right one and pounded on the door of JR's house with it while I yelled his name. I waited for the street sweeper and the traffic to calm a bit. I noticed his air conditioner was on. Surely he would not hear me. More yelling his name, this time higher, shriekier, to cut through the lulling white noise and cool air of his room, where he was probably only four hours into slumber. His head popped out from around a fan in the living room window. "Hi, buddy!" It is good he was home, as my other option was Matt, at his new job down at City Hall.

JR came outside with my keys and told me the dream he'd just had, about how human flight had been made possible and we were jumping from planes and landing safely on the ground. I tucked my keys into my pocket and headed home. I went shoeless most of the way. I wondered if the old people on their porches in my old neighborhood recognized me and wondered what sort of terrible fate had befouled me to set me pacing Oakley Avenue shoeless with my bedhead cowlick pointing towards the sky. I wondered if people thought I was just a sloppy person, or if I was on a particularly shameful walk of shame.

When I passed the church a second time, the boy was still there. We made eye contact as I was putting the shoes back on to cross the street.

I kept checking for the keys in my pocket. As a kid, I lost my house keys all the time. I spent most of my sixth grade after-school hours waiting on the porch of my parents' home. I lost my keys so often that I had to go to a therapist because it was believed perhaps I was doing it on purpose. I told the therapist the only truth: it had nothing to do with my parents' divorce. I was just disorganized and forgetful, my school bag was a mess of unfinished homework and half-eaten lunches and tapes. Plus, why would I want to be locked out of my own house? My explanation apparently sufficed and I was not made to return to further investigate the issue of chronic key loss with a professional.

Alas! I returned home, keyed and bedraggled, and realized, I could have ridden my bike, and I needn't have gone into the hall looking for the cat in the first place, as he was trapped in the closet.

June 23, 2009

'TIL GONZO DO US PART

[At stoplight, Chicago and Ashland, 1:10 a.m., on bikes.]

I need to get on that, get a summer romance going before the end of summer.

Well, then, it'll be a fall romance.

I think if I apply myself, it's possible.

What about that girl, on the bike there?

She's a touch young.

So? She's really beautiful. Look at her.

Yeah.

Start placing Missed Connections for people who may not exist.

This is your de facto advice now. You suggested the same method to Dave.

Yeah. It'll work eventually. It's got to.

How about this: "I saw you. Mecca Fashions. Me: guy buying white sport coat. You: woman trying on XL Tweety-Bird-As-Notorious-B.I.G. airbrushed T-shirt. Would like to pump semen into you immediately."

Yeah, I think that'll do it.

[Light changes. We roll towards home.]

July 24, 2008

NEW DAY RISING

You know how some nights you leave the house wanting to milk summer for all it's worth, but all you get is a good glimpse at the rotten soul of the universe as it exists in and outside of yuppie jizz discos?

So out of desperation, you and your friends go to the bar you hate trying to make good on your efforts, and the vibe is like an episode of *Cheaters* and everyone is acting like the James Spader character in an '80s teen drama, and you sit there sucking down your ice water thinking, I put on shoes for *this*?!

You walk home with your best friend, each carrying an end of your bent-up bike, trying to remember the chronology of the Hüsker Dü discography and it's all the lame fun you need right there. Aging loners waxing nerdy in the night light.

July 07, 2007

TIE A YELLOW RIBBON 'ROUND THE OL' APPLE TREE

I almost fell out of the apple tree twice on Saturday, mid–picking handoff. I was balanced on the limbs, but I caught myself on a rope. It's a good thing that Ian did not catch me or break my fall below. He had a buck knife in his hand. Ian is Robin's beau. He is a poet. Robin says he is working on a poem about Mary Poppins right now. Robin sells umbrellas for a living. Together we picked apples.

All weekend was poems and poets. In the Didion book, in discussion with Ian, in discussion with JR and Ian and Robin and Miles about Frank O'Hara and his death. I asked rhetorically and got no answer, what would it feel like to run over a great poet, to kill a great poet with a dune buggy? (Or conversely, how is death, drunk under the wheel of an ATV? Sheesh). Robin and Ian and I sat outside a rotted-out corpse of a corn maze, picnicking on snacks, and I offered that I never read poetry until 9/11, and for the next three years, it was all I read. Poems and magic realism. Normal books could not hold me, because the context seemed to have shifted and I wanted radical love, peace, disgust, outrage, and effluvial words for it. The breath-stealing lines: in Brooks's *A Street in Bronzeville,* Nikki Giovanni's bomb drop of "I am not an easy woman to want," Ginsburg imploring America to take its clothes off, five times through *The Panther & the Lash*, Wanda Coleman saying love is a pimp just the same, Ferlinghetti's "slopes of heaven," which makes me think god lives in Tuscany.

Other than apples and poems, the weekend was one of revisions and remittance, and the reluctant humility involved in both. I bought a road bike for forty bucks from the bike collective in lieu of getting a car, battling my idea of what a car provides. But what I know: in Chicago, a bike is faster than a car, and so I am seeing what happens now, seeing what happens when I commit to becoming a nondriver. Because at a certain point, the question becomes, if I am not living my most hopeful politics at the advanced age of twenty-nine, then what am I doing?

October 17, 2005

WATERMELON IN A BOX/CAT ON
THE LADDER

I lit the yard torches in hopes it would be a bat signal, or work like the search lights that roll up through the clouds so that you know where the club is, or that the Eagles are playing. (When you become that level of famous, are rolling search beacons in your production rider, or do they travel with you?) Miles worked the flammables department and then dipped to a Chicago Ave. burrito hut with my other helpmeet, JR. So I sat in the yard, alone, feet up on the table, empresaria of the ratty yard, waiting for someone to show.

No one will come. I know it. Hostess anxiety.

And then Robin, new friend, showed up. She brought champagne, cupcakes she had made, and cigarettes. Then Kiki and Doug. Then Miles and JR returned with tacos and king cans, and then more people and then some more: Hunter with his Frenchy moustache and Jane with her perfume. And then it was midnight and I was manning a watermelon that was so big that cutting it was a two-person job, and then the guest of honor, Amy (new to town), showed and it was introductions all around. It was party stories: about the dude with a watermelon on his head shitting in the yard at the Dillinger Four party, or the time JR's old roommate tossed a lit quarter-stick of dynamite out the window, six stories down and fifteen feet over from his yuppie ass neighbors' 4th of July party, cratering the blacktop. I ladled lemonade from a five-gallon bucket into red Solo cups and said, "Good to see you, good to see you."

I made the rounds and offered up laptop-sized hunks of watermelon from a Priority Mail box. Someone put my cat Monkee on top of a ladder, and people gathered around, marveled at her sweetness, her collar-with-a-bell.

August 07, 2005

THERE IS A LIGHT ON MY BIKE
THAT NEVER GOES OUT

We were off to Edmar, which is decrepit, Polish, and smells like only old grocery stores smell—a little mildew, a little grandma cologne, and the musk of coriander. They are open 'til midnight and mostly sell jarred food. I got a hazelnut-ridden candy bar for a dollar; it was very big and thick like those kinds I used to sell in order to get to go on class trips back in junior high. In the lot, I noticed for the first time, on my new/old bike, that I had one of those friction light generators, same as on my roommate Cris's bike. The same kind of light that three minutes before I was calling magic. And voilá, it turned out I had one, too!

I flicked the friction maker on the back into its lockspot and with a mouthful of chocolate and a quick start, I illuminated my path into the wet Chicago night. "I'm shining!" I yelled to Cris and reached out to give her a mini-brick of the bar. We rode towards home, pulling the tinfoil off the candy and devouring it, powering our tiny lights in tandem. Cris would just hold out her hand and say, "More." I was so happy.

As happy as I'd ever been. I told the man in the Jeep at the stop sign, "We have lights on our bikes!" because I wanted him to notice, to not miss the opportunity to witness such safety and inventiveness in motion. I got all the way home (four blocks) and realized I could not be home—I had to go power the light some more.

Every time I saw someone I knew, I stopped, offered them a square of chocolate, and showed off the glow of my new light. "See!" They would eat the treat and then head in or out of the bar door, congratulating me on my newfound luminescence. I ran into Telo, who was going into the Kill Hannah "Halfway to Halloween" 18+ dance party at the nouveau Italian restaurant. She coaxed me in. Over approximately seven minutes, I drank a water, wondered why every girl in the place thought a push-up bra/corset and underpants with a pair of Skechers was a costume, heard the Killers for the first time, and bummed a cigarette I only took two drags of from a daddy goth who rocked both a sparkly cowboy hat and Shari Lewis's eyelashes. He called me "babe" and made that clicking sound like he was goddamn Telly Savalas.

I checked out some asses and got back on my bike.

I did not mean to stop at the bar with the big open windows where everyone looks good and seems wasted, but they yelled my name, beckoned me over. They were celebrating new tattoos and twenty-third birthdays and dogs they loved and drinking "to Berlin!" with many small bottles of champagne. I gave them my last candy squares. Then, from around the doorway, a boy I spent six years with appeared; he was working the door. "You have treats?" he asked.

"Nope, those were my last ones," I said. It was not supposed to be weird, but it was. I think he thought I was just being vindictive for that time he ruined 1997–2002. I held up the empty wrapper for evidence. "Sorry!"

I hopped back on my bike, waved to the faded, and floated home, my little light showing the way.

May 10, 2005

TH' EMPIRE WEAKEND

Our monthly hang is a craft night. Valentine's edi-
tion, War of Girled-craft. The foot of snow kept a
few people at home, but those that showed glued it
up past midnight. JR was on foot and close by, so
he arrived early and immediately pressed me with a
question that was baffling him: "I heard about this
band Vampire Weekend. Someone told me that they
sound like Paul Simon—like Graceland-era—is this
true?!" I told him it was—Nassau gone Hamptons—I
have Mp3'd proof, dog. He was incredulous: "WHAT
THE FUCK?!" JR works a swing shift and doesn't
have a computer or an iPod, so he's a good gauge of
how East Coast rages and internet phenomena trans-
late (or don't) in the real world.

Despite Max starting to crawl two days ago, Robin
made it over for our first craft time since before he
was born. Robin and I have embarked on many am-
bitious and rarely finished projects, including a dog-
shaped purse, which was fondly eulogized last night:
she sewed the straps on wrong, in such a way that you
could not open the purse. Poor hermetically sealed,

too-small canvas dog. Then she bested our best work (living room curtains) by making Max. She told me I had made a monster by showing Ian how to use Hype-Machine last time I was at their house. She said all the songs he downloads are people singing, "Where's my cocaine?" or, "How come you didn't tell me you have cocaine?" and asked me to explain. I couldn't. We all came up listening to punk and hxc bands that were either too obtuse or high on moral absolutes to ever sing openly about doing drugs. We all came up in the heroin age that followed the '80s punk coke rager, and saw enough death and stolen record collections that broadcasting a drug habit—in song—is kind of beyond the pale.

AnnieLaurie, after a long day teaching bright young things at the Art Inst., came home and pounded out a grip of 'tines. She was also nice enough to share her color transparencies of diseased tissues and colons and stuff. Kelly made us a valentine for the house, "Sup Romance." Her "Welcome Homo" sign is still up on the front door, its pipe cleaners standing in stark contrast to my neighbors' country-style seasonal wreaths. JR, who is currently reading his twenty-third book on Honest Abe, made a Lincoln-tine for his room. The quote on the bottom is about conquering your enemies by turning them into friends.

I mostly shellacked feathers and glue to stuff, though my crude embellishment of a picture of a woman eating a chocolate éclair repulsed my co-creationists. Whatever, man. It's a feminist critique; I just fully illustrated what the picture implied, filled in that male gaze with some glitter and glue.

February 02, 2008

THE DANCE FLOOR IS MY PASTURE

Rolled solo to the first Friday at the MCA. Ben and Johnny were DJing, so I got listed, which was a plus; I saw the otherwise 'spensive exhibits for free and ate copious amounts of cheese cubes and nasty little egg rolls off baby plates. My favorite exhibit was the cardboard constructed Swiss chalet, comprising four tomb-rooms with Egyptian iconography, several hundred rolls of duct tape, homemade bongs, and graphic depictions of anal penetration as a comment on how America is laying waste to Iraq.

In the main room of the chalet, there was a bank of TVs playing loops of war and porn footage. Which was not my favorite part of the exhibit: watching a room full of dudes trying really hard to pretend they were not entranced by it was. Their manic minisecond glimpsing of it was comical and compelling. They would browse the cardboard pyramids and then, suddenly, jerk their heads, like startled animals, to peek at the porn, so as not to be noticed by their dates and everyone else in the room.

After that, Ben's pigtailed sis Becca and I got interviewed and had our pictures taken for the fashion section of the *Tribune*, despite the fact that I was wearing men's dress socks with gold cha-cha heels. There was a notes-taking lady, then the main lady with the tape recorder and the photographer, also taking notes. They asked me where I got my shoes, and I told them, "Some scabby-ass yuppie resale shop up north," *and they wrote it down, as if it were a hot tip.*

Got on the "dancefloor," or rather, *dominated* the blank dancing area, with a fresh new dance/solo movement exhibition I was doing to amuse Ben and Johnny. It's called the Hungry Pony and it goes like this: stamp the ground, pawing the floor three times left, then three times right. Hands up like you're about to catch a basketball. Mime a sort of cud-chewing motion, opening and closing your mouth to the beat of the song, or you can also eat for real. Stare blankly at anyone who even so much as glances at you.

The Hungry Pony got some good reactions, and is an easy fit with everything from J.J. Fad to French house to King Tubby. A fifty-something doctor man came over and said, "What you are doing is great. The dress you are wearing, its Asian style combined with your dancing, you are like a Kabuki donkey. Your dress is great, by the way." He toasted me with his glass and walked away. Another guy pawed the floor back at me, with the subtlety of a drug deal signal. I showed the dance to Johnny's friend, who deals in soybean futures and had on a green chapeau, and his friend the internet clothing magnate. They told me I was the funniest person they had ever met, which means either they were way drunker than they let on, or this dance is much more genius than I ever intended.

April 02, 2005

THE MIRACLE OF REINVENTION

You are older and you think you are settled in who you are but a new city and sitch in extremis can mute you. Dave said tonight, "The other night in the car, I realized that maybe we're not seeing all sides of you." The other side being my naturally dominant crass and caustic side. The moment he was referencing was Friday night, five of us packed in a car, driving to West Covina to play an improvisational noise set at a house show, when the taciturn stranger in the front seat mentioned he was from a midwestern city I have little love for. I said emphatically, "Really?! That place is a shithole!" and laughed. Everyone else was silent for about fifteen seconds. *I was joking*, I said. *It's not that bad*. Damien offered up a consolation: "Well, that arch thing is neat." Yes, yes it is. It's a fucking miracle of modern engineering—but if mocking suburban St. Louis is profane, lord help me.

I'm coming home to Chicago by mid-month; all I want is to ride bikes and have Nora and Morgan regale me with the nastiest, most offensive jokes they can conjure, maybe Ben can meet me at the airport with a big banner that says "WELCOME HOME FUCKFACE"—'cos I gotta shake these West Coast propriety blues.

July 02, 2008

LET'S GET OUT WHILE THE GETTING'S GOOD

To steal from John and Exene: I'm not buying a lamp on Hollywood Blvd. the day I leave, but it does feel sad. Sort of. Almost. Not really. I'm coming home. Soon. I think.

California skim milk skies'll still hang heavy over the 5 whether I'm here to witness or no. I'm filling my dad's freezer with chickens I made so that he doesn't get Nicole Richie–slender while I'm gone.

I just need to go home and stare into Tito's furry face and cry with love, stare into all my friends' faces and cry with love, finish a manuscript, ride around listening to Adina Howard tapes on bikes wiff Ben til 4 a.m., sleep not on the floor, stand atop the train bridge facing east and channel the ghost of Sandburg's bowtie to purge my mortal fears, go rest my face on the cool granite floors of the empty atrium atop Harold Washington Library, kiss a copy of *Neon Wilderness* three times for luck and ask god what's next.

July 09, 2008

TOP DOWN RIMS SPINNIN'

David came straight from O'Hare in this sweet ride, a rented Chrysler Sebring with Wisconsin plates, and scooped me, JR, and Morgo right up. Our Stephen Stills Appreciation Brunch, usually relegated to my dining room, instead went on beach-cation to the Hawaii of Indiana™. JR brought some esoteric Turkish disco, I brought a Zep/Metallica CD I burned, and since we roll driver's choice, my choice prevailed. He did not mind. On the way home we put on *Exile in Guyville* and the boys sang every word, explaining all they came to understand from it. Then we picked up Nora, who insisted on getting in and out of the car Dukes-style, clambering over the side. Whenever we saw someone we knew while we were driving, she'd yell: "IT'S A RENTAL!"

July 25, 2008

KEYS TO THE CITY VERSUS
532 WORDS OF FAME

I ain't smoked a cigarette in four days, and I knew visiting club land with Miles would be temptation island. But we were in and out, strolling simply on some return-the-favor shit, a karmic reboot, giving face time at the *other* marginally attended monthly DJ nights around town. Support Your Local Scene.

I was wearing a long knit poncho that is a Neil Young for Girls model from the thrift, mostly purple and stripes. I like to wear it when I am about on the bike 'cause it makes a good shadow, makes me look like a bird, arcing long across the ground between streetlights, fringe as feathers. It conjures a superheroic feel. Apparently, no one else is getting this vibe, as two separate pairs of drunk lubbers a mere block apart called out to me, asking for "pot." Both times the people made a squinchy face and mimed a *puff-puff-pass*. Both times the men asking for weed had wet-looking hair and untucked black dress shirts over light-rinse denim jeans. Perhaps someone posted a note on Craigslist that around bar-close on weeknights an elf-sized girl in a purple cape rides down Chicago Avenue, tossing lids of fine Humboldt County bud out of her front-mounted plastic bike basket. They must have been standing there waiting for their drop, and got me confused with her.

It was a funny thing—funny "haha" and "god's handiwork" funny—tonight when, after ol' Al B. stopped by for catch-up and tea and grilled cheeses, we went off to Kinkos. He to xerox his new comic book and me to pick up the mini-reissues of *Hit It or Quit It* that I had printed up. They are twelve years old, their masters are crumbly and stained, with brittle ancient tape around the edges and grunge's cruel irrelevance. On the way home, I stopped and picked up the *Reader* with my first piece in it. I was carrying these two stacks into the house when I realized they were the exact bookends of my writing life. The little fanzine I brought to the Uptown Kinkos in Minneapolis in 1991, because no magazine or paper or monthly shill sheet would let me write for them—and like magic, here, thirteen years after the fact, I am finally living my teenage dream.

April 01, 2005

BUH-BYE

My friends Roby and Rjyan are returning to the place where the streets are paved with Jackin House mixes: Baltimore. Tonight I stood in the back of their moving truck with my arms un-sleeved, a skin-showing ode to today's high of fifty-seven, just doing a little soft-shoe to stay warm. They had been trying to ring me to tell me, but by the time they reached me, well, the announcement was, "We're moving. To Baltimore. Tomorrow." So I went over to help, to guard the truck while they ran up and down the three flights piling in everything they owned except furniture: Puppet theatre. Cassettes. A loom. Power tools. An eight-track recorder wrapped in a sleeping bag. Cat habitat. A medium-sized pony from an amusement ride. Buckets of house paint.

They would slide it in, and I would arrange it. I tap-tap-tapped in their absence and thought about how every time I move, I get closer and closer to getting rid of all my cassettes. Am down to ten precious cassettes documenting the moments of the nineties that still hold romance. Thought about every time I moved cross country like fire, ditching everything save for my seven inches, my favorite shoes, my typewriter, and my ferocious emotional calamity. Remembered driving through New Mexico, en route from Minneapolis to LA, in the middle of the night, listening to Sonic Youth *Evol*, buzzed on the trucker speed that came complimentary with the ancient Econoline van I was driving, overjoyed and scared shitless, because I had graduated from high school the week before and now my life was wide open for me to really fuck up.

They left behind magic stuff I could not take: a collection of choir robes, a steamer trunk, ladders, a bag of butterscotch chips, raincoats, and a curtain made from a wedding dress found in the trash. I did get a drawer, a tiara, some potted violets, all their tea, rice, garbanzo beans, nutmeg nuts, a collection of tiny jars they had painted the words "true love" on, and the backdrop from one of Roby's puppet shows that takes place in a foreign land. It's a handsewn tapestry of a downtown with a big red velvet castle. I did not take their collection of corks, but I was tempted to.

I will miss them terribly, Rjyan and Roby, especially come summer, come bike weather. I will miss watching them being halves of the great thing they have become. I do not begrudge them the sudden move, as sometimes you just have to bail.

March 29, 2005

OH, YOU KNOW. FINE.

I got a couple emails this week saying, "Are you ok? I have been reading your blog. How are you, *really*?" All the people who ask are on the coasts and most definitely enduring winter differently from those of us who rock $270 monthly heating bills here in the 312. I went to the record store today, to do some bartering and trading, and I whispered to my friend, the clerk, "I am thinking maybe I should buy those Bright Eyes albums, what's up with that?" He did not have an answer. I asked the three other clerks I knew how they were, and all of them answered, "Ah, you know. Fine, I guess." This is my dispatch saying, if you live here, you understand. Everyone is feeling the deep funk of winter's bitch turn.

Most of my friends are content to drink and fuck it off or turn it from a Blockbuster night into a Blockbuster week. I do not have those obliteration lifestyle choices. I do not drink, the man I smooch is on tour, and I got hella fines at Earwax and can only rent when that kid from Mahjongg is working because he does not care about my $46 late fee.

So, I use disco records like drugs, nurse my water (light on the ice, please) at the tumbleweed-populated DJ nights my friends do, stomp out crop circles in the snow while on my 3 a.m. smoke break, wait for the *New Yorker* to show, play tricks on the cat, spend a few hours unfreezing the pipes with a hairdryer every couple days, stare directly at the sun when I can with the hope it releases some narcotic-level serotonin into my skull, and imagine life in equatorial climes where I drive a car made from coconuts and am accompanied by a fez-wearing spider monkey who keeps me amused by signing dirty jokes and playing the accordion.

So, you know, fine. Fine. I guess.

January 21, 2005

VULTURABILITY

Even though it might mean I bounce those seven massive pre-dated checks I sent to the IRS last week, I went and bought some comics today, as Quimby's was having their annual blowout zine backstock sale. I bought the new *Hamster Man Anthology* and the new Anders Nilsen comic, *Dogs and Water*.

Anders Nilsen. I get mortifyingly embarrassed every time I see him, since discovering four years ago he was my neighbor. I recognized him as he was xeroxing *Big Questions* comics next to me at Kinkos. I sweated for about seventeen minutes before turning to him and saying, "Hey, did you go to South?" Which I knew the answer to. Of course he went to South. He was three years ahead of me: Anders, my first punk rock boy crush. I still remember the inscription beneath his senior photo, thirteen years after the fact: "What the Replacements said." Everyone else had shout-outs to Danceline co-captains, inside jokes, and mentions of people they would always remember. And, just like in high school, he still has no idea who I am.

"We went to a Babes in Toyland show together in 1991," I explained, and introduced myself. I left out all the other details that might truly jog his memory: I was about four feet tall and purposefully took the same ceramics class as him, in which I spent several months making pinchpot ashtrays and staring at him. I had braces, a middle part, wore tunics and cowboy boots, and owned a wide array of Mudhoney and the Fluid T-shirts. Neither ninth grade nor grunge fashion were kind to me.

He remembered our mutual friends, but not me. He remembered the show, too, the record release for the *To Mother* EP. I had never moshed at a show before. We stood on the edge of the "the pit," and I wanted to really seem down, like some old pro, so I started bumping, periodically and rather roughly, into Anders. I was trying to show off that like, yeah, I go to punk shows and mosh it up allllll the fucking time, man. Of course I achieved the exact opposite, sporadically bumping into someone who was standing *completely and totally still*. After maybe the fifth time, he looked down at me and said, "What are you doing?" Oh, it was just the worst.

November 27, 2004

WHERE THE ATOM GOT SPLIT

I was so tired of talking. By the end of the day, the story got much shorter. The ending changed every twelve minutes, so really, why bother. And every ending gave new color to the story, so I just gave myself to the idea that history is fluid, and as much as we like things to be permanent and fixed, it's all just motion, and until perspective comes, well, it's just information.

By 11 p.m., I was standing at the place where the atom got split. The sculpture marking the former site of Fermilab, below where the U of C football field was. I imagined an atomic explosion occurring on the thirty-yard line, one that would only exist in a teen gross-out movie—a severed hand would land in the horn of a tuba.

The sculpture marking the atom split looks like a skull, a phi, the innards of a door lock. Little marks slicing out like sunrays on the ground. As a sculpture, it makes a lot of sense. As a sculpture, it is easy. I said to Miles, "I want to make things like this, but I know I do not have the patience or the tenacity. See all the etched marks on this side? I wouldn't have made it that far. I'm just not that kind of person."

We were thirsty, so we bailed from the contemplative spot.

Miles smoked, I spit, we barely spoke.

I said, "Look at that."

He said, "Look at this."

October 12, 2004

WORST IDEAS TAKEN TO THE NEXT LEVEL

Tonight, at the Buddy loft, Ashland and Katie and Liz and I made the Muy Romantico video, which does not feature any member of the band, for inclusion on the Diesel DVD that you will get free when you buy some jeans. It will no doubt fit, next to, oh . . . a Shins video. In keeping with the *Dogme 95*–style aesthetic, the modus of Muy Romantico's album production methods, and the aesthetic rule of "first idea = best idea/worst idea = best idea," we shot only about twenty-two minutes of tape. We posted on Friendster, inviting people to show up at the park on bikes/skateboards/roller skates at 11. Ten people RSVP'd and one showed. That was Katie, who had roller-skated about two miles from her house. Ashland brought two hair school mannequin heads which he had scalped, so they were half-wearable. Meaning they only fit about a third of the way over our heads. Katie's wore headphones, and mine was adorned with an "I Love Reggae" sweatband that Miles brought me from Negril.

As per Ashland's nondirection, we skated with the rubber heads on, which was interesting as we could not see. Minimal injuries after I skated into a bench. Then we did some high-speed backwards skating while taking off layer upon layer of clothes and talking on our cell phones until we were down to T-shirts in the forty-one-degree weather. It was as terrible as it sounds. We came back inside, filmed Ashland *licking* the rubber heads, changed into more "video-type" outfits (unicorn sweatshirts, excessive gold jewelry, ratted hair), then drove to pick up Liz, who was wearing two concha belts and a tie-dyed shirt and cut-off jean shorts and a dreamcatcher for an earring. Wearing roller skates while driving may be the most stupidly dangerous thing I have done, at least since the time I drove wearing ice skates. We then went to the trendy local yuppie bar, where we were planning on crawling on the floor (à la Duran Duran's "Rio" video), but Jeff Parker was there free-jazzing it, which kind of ruined the vibe, so we just roller-skated in the bathroom, staged some slow-motion crashes, and left and headed to the grocery. Upon entering, the manager met us at the door and said, "You cannot wear skates in the store," and Liz goes, "Ok, thanks . . . GO!" We took off full-speed down the frozen foods aisle with Ashland running behind us, made a lap through the store, and exited without being busted by the totally confounded staff.

Tomorrow, we drop the tape off with Dave, and we have only allotted him ninety minutes to edit it.

My guess is it will be ruthlessly shitacular genius.

That's all you can really hope for in this life anyway, right?

April 02, 2004

GLOBAL WARMUPS

Still reading/rereading Mamet—more helpful snaps for New Year's resolutions. His sister's line in "True Stories of Bitches," when he complains about eating the pastrami sandwich he ordered: "You are a fool"—she was saying "you are a fool to be eating food you disapprove of. Your inability to rule your life according to your perceptions is an unfortunate trait." At the White/Light show last night, inside and outside in the smokers' line under the overhang, people complained about resolutions on habits not being held to. Doing stuff they didn't want to be doing, because the tide of their life and habits was taking them there, taking them on dates with dudes who were a-holes. Perhaps it's time for one big holistic resolution: shorten an impossible-to-manage, epic list of feelings and actions to be curtailed or expanded, and pledge, simply, to quit ordering the proverbial pastrami sandwich you hate!

Also, the Julie Doucet book, *365 Days*, is hard to put down. Not because of a feeling of anticipation about what will happen next, but because of what won't. I have always felt that true artists surely adhere to a rigorous path that doesn't look terribly like normal life. You know, solitude and tortured drinking, sensual fete-ing all the livelong day, breach-birthing ideas, untenable discipline. But reading Doucet's diary of 2002–03, it is the routine of it that is familiar and comforting. The boon of worth and productivity she feels when she gets a check in the mail. Hovering just above poverty. Slogging through creative lulls, wanting things to be exciting. Being envious of the ease of other people's creative successes. It's reassuring and inspiring that you don't have to be Mark Rothko—pacing and cursing and suicidal—in order to be an artist.

January 08, 2008

"BANGING LIKE G. GORDON LIDDY"

JR spent his thirtieth birthday with me this week, despite the fact that he works SEVEN DAYS A WEEK (you wanna see shitty job market, whiny freelancer? Come to Chicago and see all the best writers I know restocking hangers in the Juniors Department at H&M, tooth-and-nailing for a way out—no shit) and currently spends his evenings reading *Moby-Dick*. He hung out, let me steal his cigarettes and gossip about my dumb life, and said, "You know, when NASA wants to send something to Mars, they have to shoot it around the moon. Right now, you're sling-shotting around the moon." And then took a drag of his Marb lite and flipped to ESPN2 for highlights.

March 31, 2004

BUMPING TO BONNIE TYLER

I took off on the bike into the Chicago fake spring, and every three blocks pulled up to the curb to say hello to people I knew, out in their dapper weekend wear, clasping their lover's hand, making a trail for the smoky bar. Everyone I met and spoke with today, barring Julianne, was a touch wasted, starting with my sister, whom I picked up from O'Hare this morning after her eight-day college spring break trip to Miami. She returned with extra sunburn on one side of her face, puffy, knotty, platinum hair, no voice and no shoes.

An hour later, my bandmate Dave called and asked if I had seen Al. Apparently, after taking some super potent shamanistic hallucinogens, Al attempted to leave the house naked. They managed to get his clothes back on him, but then he slipped out the door undetected moments later. Al told me later at band practice, "For forty minutes I was overwhelmed by the falseness of the universe. I saw everything as it was—paved over. Everything became Lego-like. Cigarette smoke and wearing clothes seemed like my biggest enemies." Totally.

Mid–bike ride, I ran into Dave and Al and Lauren, leaving a party with pink teeth, a wide slosh in their steps, and pockets of fancy Euro candy pilfered from Lauren's advisor's ritzy party. (This being the Midwest, any party that does not have a keg of Pabst in the corner is "fancy.") I walked them home the few blocks, smoked Dave's cigarettes and stole a cup of water, while Dave regaled us with new stories of their Jr. Eminem neighbor, under house arrest next door, who, because of his ankle decoration, stands on the porch of his mother's house, begging any and all passing for company. He just got out of jail for stealing the other next-door neighbor's car. Dave's drunken genius went like this: "What sort of mother are you if you are screaming at your son, 'You *mother*fucker,' like, twelve times a day? Does she know the implications?"

March 28, 2004

I REMEMBER WHEN I MET YOU

Last night, Miles and I went to the Hold Steady show, and we were psyched. As were some diehards and some new fans and some people from Detroit. All in attendance yelled and hooted and mewled at Craig Finn, who sang to us, tales of a last-call wonderland, one hundred kinds of hopeless, and Jesus, too. ("Jesus rolled his eyes when his dad made Jesus jokes / he forgave me for my sins / he said let this famine end and let the two-for-ones begin.")

The only picture I have of Craig was taken on the front lawn of my parents' former home in Minneapolis. It was the week after I graduated from high school, and my parents had gone on vacation and I was having a yard sale, selling all the clothes and records I had to fund my move to LA the following week. The picture of Craig marks an exact wrong turn in my young life. I was heading to LA to be with a boyfriend. While Craig was standing there, the boyfriend called; I had not heard from him in two weeks. He told me he was in love and getting married. To a woman he had met three weeks earlier. Who was thirty-six. They were shooting drugs and living in a motel on Sunset and he said he hoped I could be happy for him. Craig made the kind suggestion that maybe I not move to LA in light of this development. I took his picture. I moved to LA anyway. I stayed for three months, where I shaved my head and took to wearing old-lady wigs, slips, and a fake fur coat to shows. I moved back to Minneapolis the week after my eighteenth birthday, and then moved back to LA four days after Bob Stinson died, later that winter.

The last time I saw Tad, the bassist for the Hold Steady, we were in the backyard of some dude from D4 in St. Paul somewhere, and everyone was wasted or high except for me. I was wearing a shawl and Tad asked me why I was dressed like "fucking Stevie Nicks." I told him he had more in common with Stevie Nicks than I did. Tad and I never really got along. I was barely paying attention to him because there was a dude behind him with half a hollowed-out watermelon over his head, running around the yard with his pants around his ankles. Later on, perhaps without the melon on, he was trying to shit under a tree and someone stole his pants. The only person who would help him was his girlfriend, and she left in tears shortly after.

The first time I met Miles, I was babysitting the door for a minute for a show at the Empty Bottle. In maybe 1999. I know this story mostly because Miles told me. Miles asked who I was, despite knowing; he had read my fanzine and recognized me. I told him my name was Jambalaya. A few minutes later, Miles stepped into the photo booth next to the door, and in the second shot, my arm appears above his head, flipping him off. He has the picture to prove it. Miles used to be DJ Innocent Bloodshed (back when we used to advertise him as "from Detroit," even though he's from Kalamazoo), but then he came up with a new name so we sound like a brother/sister DJ team: DJ Yves St. Le Roc. Despite the fact that his writing is just unbeatable, Miles, along with several of my good friends, works in the Young Trend department at H&M.

That is all I remember.

March 12, 2004

THE INEXPLICABLE

Ben and I went to dinner this evening, despite me
being so high on Theraflu my side of the conversation was like a Fluxus happening. Ben's sister was
our waitress, and I kept ordering cigarettes from her
to take the medicine's speedy edge down a notch,
complimenting her on her soft arm skin and kiss-
ing her cheek every time she came by to freshen up
Ben's whiskey. She obliged me, returning thrice with
purloined Gauloises, so I tipped her 65 percent, and
later spent fifteen minutes trying to explain to her the
phenomenon of cat dancing, and cats who can paint,
and how I am fantasizing about developing a Walk-
man for animal use.

Many people greeted us through the course of the
meal, starting with my ex-boyf's ex-roommate, who,
mistaking Ben for my ex-boyf, hugged Ben from
behind in a way that men who have not previously
shared a home bathroom do not do. Ben had no idea
who he was. Both were nervous and startled, accidentally interlocked in a boldly sensual way. I forgot

about my tilapia tacos and ate the shredded white radishes and mango salsa with my fingers while Ben and I gossiped as only publicists can gossip. We are in charge of all the secrets.

From there we went to the Rainbo. All of our friends who work in the area came in as their shifts at the record stores and cafes expired. Lindsey and her boyfriend came in. She looked very Butterfield 8, with pearl earrings and a terrifically partied-out hotness to her. She threw herself into the booth next to me, tugged her coat off, and declared her absolute wastedness from hours at a work function. She put her face up to my face, and in a slurry sing-song she declared that she had stopped in so her man could buy her more "al-kuh-haul." She stood up to show off her black silk crepe dress that made her look all the more alabaster. She then showed me her fresh pink manicure and her shoes, which she removed, and hoisted her leg above the tabletop so we could witness the perfection of her glossy red pedicure through her white fishnets. Then she raised her dress to her hips to show off her garters, which had bows on them. Then she laughed like she was flirting with herself, stood and threw herself into the arms of her boyfriend, and kissed him like she was going to eat him.

March 04, 2004

bauds, shows,
water with ice

FAKE SUMMER WITH REAL SNOW

After uncrunkling from the plane ride back to Chicago, I nabbed Miles and Ben and we made our way to the summer-themed dance party at the old-man Polish bar on Division. Dressed for summer, you got in for three dollars; you had to pay an eight-dollar fine for dressing "winter." We all were wearing parkas but slid in for three a pop. I don't think Miles even paid because he was rocking this unholy look that he termed "Marc Bolan as a Crip," which seemingly qualified him for the get-in-free level.

The theme party was rife with the boozy and braless. The combo of sunglasses indoors, halter tops, Top-40 music, and inflatable plastic palm trees summoned images of every '80s movie party scene where the parents are out of town. Or, perhaps, Chuck Klosterman's birthday party, staged at a Sandals resort.

Ben and I slunk down into a booth, Miles mingled. I nursed my tap water on the rocks, Ben his Bud brown bottle. After six minutes, somewhere in the bridge of

"Lean Back," our eyes glued with glum fascination to the freed asses of the partytown's real party girls, Ben turned and said, "You know, it really is true what they say about white girls and dancing." I slurped a yes out of my straw and continued with my mute origami folding of the waxy Tootsie Roll wrappers on the table. I thought about all the other things I'd rather be doing, like catching up on back issues of the *New Yorker* or fucking my boyfriend.

I only like summer parties during the real summer. These winter parties are like a joke with no punchline.

Stayed another forty minutes, by apathy and by accident, a result of having an interminable string of ninety-second conversations with people whose names I should know by now. They all seemed surprised to see me and inquired about what I am doing in town, which made me feel both hermetic and worldly, as if spending a few weeks at a time in Minnesota were equivalent to "living abroad." It is, perhaps, the deepest dream come true of most notorious me: no one actually thinks I live here anymore.

Things livened up considerably once Ralph, DBA Major Taylor, hit the decks. It's nice to feel the skilled caress of a DJ who cuts the hit by the bridge and gets you to the next song, better than the last. No fourteen seconds of silence followed by a techno remix of an ironic and terrible pop song that indicates the DJ cannot actually tell the difference between good techno and bad techno because it's all just "dance" music to them. And that's usually followed by the forever shit-sandwich of Billy Idol/the Rapture/the Cars—all the bands that make me wish for Old-Testament god to hurry up and exact his wrath on us already. All this more than made up for opening his set with "O.P.P," which I view as the sort of song you only play at wedding receptions when the barf-drunk bridesmaids are shoeless and slipping around the parquet in their nude hose.

I spent the rest of the time tonguing Tootsie Rolls out of my molars and casually watching the bathroom lines, getting angry and sad (and various toxic combinations of the two) as people I knew, including some bona fide friends, shuffled two-by-two into the men's and ladies' rooms and came out sniffing, mechanically jittery, and grinding their teeth. I abandoned my witness seat, pocketed the rest of the Tootsie Rolls, cheek-kissed those I came with, and retreated home. Watching the smart and talented trying to stave off the reality of their thirties with a Similac-cut bump really gets me down.

February 13, 2005

HONEY BUNNY

Tonight I went to this Lollapalooza fundraiser for the Chicago Parks where two-hundred-odd people paid between $350 and $15,000 to be able to sit on white leather couches in front of the Petrillo band shell and talk through Spoon's set while enjoying bottle service. Perry Farrell introduced them and big-upped the community and the good vibes of Lolla and the spirit of the fundraiser, which pays for new bushes for the city. Thanks, Perr! Shrubs for life!

Some society matrons straight out of the pages of *Sheridan Road* attempted to befriend me—Trish and Trish's friend and Mimi. Well, Mimi wasn't a matron, she was just a spunky young party gal who said she had to talk to me because she hadn't actually seen someone eating an apple "off the core" since third grade. She was really inquisitive. "Why not bananas?" she asked. Bananas don't hold up well in the purse. "Do you have celiac disease? Is that why you are eating it?" No. Apples are in season and I like them. It was a real mind-blower for her, me gnawing my apple. She also considered it a real tragedy that I don't drink.

Trish was not baffled by my apple. She walked up to me, apropos of nothing, and said, "Oh, you're here alone, too," and handed me a cigarette without me asking. Trish just wanted to hang out because watching the band would keep her from drinking and thus keep her from "getting in trouble." She and her friends just wanted to dress up, rock out, get loose, and take a night off from their kids. She poked me in the tit, in the letters spelling SONIC YOUTH on my shirt, and said, "I used to love that band." She also liked the first three Spoon songs, but not the fourth, and wondered why Britt was singing with a British accent if he's not from England. She likes Spoon 'cause they remind her of Oasis. She kept begging me to dance with her, but her version of dancing was actually just twirling, and seeing as I had just eaten, I passed. Spoon was good, but Trish and Mimi were really the highlight of the show for me.

August 03, 2007

MIXING DRINKS WITH FLATTER AND EASY CREDIT WITH YOUR DEALER

On the corner, I got a light from a guy who is also a writer. He was standing with a girl who looked like Snow White, but hotter. A guy I didn't want to talk to had followed me out of the bar, wasted, trying to talk to me. I wished for a hole to open up in the sidewalk and magically shoot me home. We all stood silent for an awkward few seconds. The men's balance tentative, they rolled from their toes to their heels, teetering like they were on the bow of an invisible ship that held only them. They were both wet-eyed and sloppy drunk, eyelids having the persistent slow slitting of the narcotized. The writer boy handled the introductions.

This is Melissa.

Actually, it's Miranda.

Melissa, this is Jeszzzzsss—

He sounds like a snake when he says it, the "s" like a slow leak.

Jessica. I shake her hand.

How do you guys know each other?

I'm a writer, he's a writer.

Jessica she's a music. Journalism. Write. She. He's trying to untangle the words, to properly conjugate "write." His eyes seem loose in their sockets. She's theee writer here.

Oh, really. That's what I want to do. Says Miranda/ Melissa.

We talk about writing, she asks for advice, I explain to her what a fanzine is.

HIT IT OR QUIT IT the other boy thunders, bowing and throwing his hand towards the sky. I know! I was there!

The writer boy interrupts.

Jessica has a blog.

It's true, I do.

I write about it sometimes. He scrunches his face down towards mine. I love it, but sometimes I have to make fun of it. He shrugs by way of apology.

It's ok. That's how I make my living too.

He turns to the girl: She's great, but lately, her blog is. Confusing?

He turns to me: No! Flat.

Back to the girl: But her paid writing. Hoo boy. Fire.

To me: Blog. Nuhsomush. He smiles nervous and hard like he's trying to keep his teeth in.

Yeah. It hasn't been a funny-fun summer. I'm lean on jokes.

He begins to backpedal: Actually can I fawn, can I explain to her who Jessica Hopper is?

I'd prefer if you didn't. He tries anyway.

Is your grandma dead now? He asks in the middle of a sentence.

No. She is still with us, thankfully.

Both of the boys are trying to jibber at us while we try to talk to one another. They are too drunk to handle the sobriety of our conversation. I hear Kathleen Hanna in my head—"tell me what the fuck we're doing here / why are all the boys acting strange" — and the girl drops the bomb.

Yeah, this has been a terrible summer. My ex-boyfriend just died and then my boyfriend dumped me right after.

Both the boys reel back. The hot girl has a just-dead boyfriend: there goes Plan A! No one is getting in her pants tonight. Their default setting is treacle-slow game spitting, but they manage to offer condolences in unison: "Whoa."

Jinx!

July 25, 2008

DEEP SAX WORKING YOUR SOUL LIKE THE ALL-NITE WENDY'S DRIVE-THRU, OR: VANDERMARK DRINKS SPRITE *ON ICE*

JR and I were leaving the Bottle, in no haste, in case the Vandermark 5 decided to fire up again, even though I could tell they were calling it a night by the way Vandermark and Fred Lonberg-Holm clasped backs and patted one another and said, "Good one, man" (I was close enough to hear the exchange, close enough even to report to you that Vandermark uses Rico sax reeds, gauge 3 ½, and drinks his Sprite on the rocks). I said to JR, "Whenever I come to these jazz nights here, I feel like I am setting myself up for an "I Saw You" ad in the back of the *Reader*—"

JR interrupted, "—*Me: guy with beard, wearing poncho*—"

I finished, "—*You: only girl at show.*"

I cry at Brötzmann shows, and I can tell you I choked up at every song—*every* song—of the second set of the V5 tonight. So maybe you'd think I was a *natural jazz crier*—I ain't. I'm not some sissy, getting salty-faced every time someone free-skronks. It's because when I see them play I am overcome with the sense that god is within both them and me.

(The first time I heard the Vandermark 5 was during a two-month period in which I was a clerk at a record store called Arons in Hollywood. We got a promo in the store of *Single Piece Flow* and it was so burly and explosive that after half a play, I was "banned" from playing it. That and the Azita solo album that came out at the same time were the first things that embedded the wondering about *what the fuck is going on there in Chicago*? I ate a dollar's worth of donut holes from Donut Time in the parking lot on my breaks in lieu of meals and plotted my way out here.)

About ten days ago, JR, laid into Matt and me because Vandermark plays like thirty-seven times a month, plays the Bottle almost every week sometimes, and we never go see him. JR said we're assholes for not paying five bucks to see a living legend. He said, "What if you, every week for years, had the chance to see Ornette but didn't? Years later you'd feel like a fool, missing the chance!"

So tonight, we went, and yes, I feel like King Asshole—JR called it. I have lived here for nine years, and fucking A, I have only seen Vandermark three times. Woe unto me and my poor judgment. The V5 hit all the right and wrong notes and seized and purred and oh, that reassuring diesel hum of the tenor.

The whole night was holy qua holy, though maybe I was listing a shade Catholic already. Spent two hours holed up at a corpo-cafe talking about god with some women I roll with. On the street I said goodbye to an old friend I hardly ever see these days. She comes out only occasionally now, revivifying in between rounds of cancer treatment. I told her my sister was home from Spain and she said, "Oh, I want my ashes scattered around the Park Güell fountain in Barcelona." I wanted to shush and reassure her not to talk like that, tell her she'll live forever, but she's fifty and has had a multitude of cancers and is allowed to strike a note of mortality in casual conversation.

We talked about the Vatican and its gaudy monuments to mortal men, and embalmed nuns in Montreal, and how she hated Catholic church as a child because of the dead waxy-faced nun in the glass case. I told her why I can't stand mass. Because they say, "Christ Jesus." It's like how gym teachers only call you by your last name, it makes me think the priest is taking attendance.

Later, over hot drinks, my friend Margaret talked about praying like you already got what you prayed for: "I didn't come up with that one. That's direct from the big guy." I love it when people call god "the big guy," like he's the manager of the Red Sox. She also recited most of "St. Patrick's Breastplate" from memory, the part that's the hymn. I like the part about doing god's work in the world, but the part about "spells of witches, smiths and wizards" is a bit much. The Smiths? Or blacksmiths? Wicked blacksmiths crafting evil horseshoes or garden gates?

The snow has melted into ashy-colored heaps and left the ground uncovered, exposing slick leaves, empties,

and months of frozen dog turds now delicately thaw-
ing. It rained but did not snow. I know these soft
winters are bad for farmers and crops, but I like the
solitude and slow pace of the bike and its baskets and
pedal-powered lights. Feels good to be in the streets
again.

December 28, 2005

ROUNDING UP (OR DOWN, DEPENDING)

I went to night three of the Blackout! Fest at the Empty Bottle over the weekend, and I forgot to tell you 'bout it. River City Tanlines, one of the many, many endeavors of the hardest-working lady in the real for real *real* underground, Alicja Trout, were worth the fifteen bucks all by themselves. While watching them play, I dreamt of a different world where Alicja is as revered as Ian MacKaye. She is in four bands, is an incredible songwriter, is a grown-up, runs a mail-order distro and a recording studio, and has this un-cocky but very tangible confidence on stage that maybe I have never seen. River City Tanlines are so raw and so pop, they make (insert any mainstream-celebrated garage band of the last five years here) sound like goddamn Chad and Jeremy singing about leaves in the wind by comparison.

Other fun facts: In the first two nights of Blackout!, the Empty Bottle went through roughly 170 cases of beer (no figure available for tap beer). Napkin math: 24 beers in each of 170 cases is 4,080 beers. Divided by 330 attendees over 2 nights, that's 12.3 beers per person. Per capita, it was the drunkest place I think I have ever been. A third of the crowd was having a great time, the other third was that weird, silent, scary drunk, and the last third was like Darby Crash–style wasted: spittle flying from broken teeth, pinballing between people and the wall as they walked past, screaming the augmented lyrics to "Grand Ole Flag" ("Hummm ov da . . . fwee! / and land ov the . . . day-ed!") before barfing into the pocket of their companion's dinner jacket.

May 23, 2005

REMINISCING: IT'S NOT JUST A LITTLE RIVER BAND SONG

Miles is right, we should have tried harder. Last time I saw Botch play in Chicago was, I think, in '99, a hardcore matinee at the Fireside. There were maybe ninety kids there and a bunch of them were mosh-jocks and Dave said something about it from the stage, about being respectful to everyone else who came to see the show and not get punched, and some kid yelled, "Shut up, Ian!" and we took it as a call to action to disrupt the pit. A minor cabal of seven or eight of us did the "rip it up" en masse, shredding the air with aerobic, clawing hands. I remember Agnew being on Justin's shoulders at some point, each of us taking turns stage-diving gently into the lofted arms of a friend, *Ice Capades*–style. An old intern of mine was there, and he had stripped down to his boxers. I dared him to take off his unders, put his socks on his hands and touch every single person in the room with his wet sock-paw. He did it, and then, unpro-voked, performed a sort of "sexy dance" in the pit, wearing nothing but a Le Tigre shirt, his shoe, and his socks still on his hands, and it was the most effective method I have ever seen to get hardcore ruffians to stop their macho violence.

December 06, 2006

GREAT, OUTDOORS

I lost the sound on Oakley, two blocks from home, so it traveled a full mile with me. Towards the end, I could only hear pockets. Passing a straight-away alley or a tall building, it would ricochet, voice tripling over eleven-second-old beats: "ESS-OOH-VEE." I passed a foundry on Fulton, dudes were on break, and I wondered, do they wonder what the alien din is? Or do they know about grime? It became another genre in the wind between the festival and my casa.

Of today: Ghostface *did* show. Two missed flights but he did show, wrapped in a towel, saying our city's name. I was a city block away, pilfering fried cheese curds from Tommy's paper basket and then a game of telephone broke out, each person relaying down the curb that we were eating on:

"The whole posse is on stage."

"There's like sixteen people on stage."

"Starks has thirty people on stage."

"That's not his posse, that's all the American Apparel hoochies."

"Dude, there's like 1,000 people on stage."

We walked slowly towards Ghostface; he did four or six songs, an ODB tribute with a tender dedication. Tommy said, "Are you allowed to do that?" and Philip, possibly serious, said, "People dedicate things to dead people all the time. Hospital wings, libraries. It's tradition." We got as far as the sound booth, and from then out, he just big-upped the White Sox, got grinded on by the approximately forty-five to sixty women onstage, and told us all, "Make your booty bounce to get your pussy wet." I asked Liz if that happens to her when she dances. She said, "Yeah. When I am dancing and thinking, 'Jeez, I look hot.' Sure." Miles said it does not happen to him.

Erase Errata were the Minutemen of the fest. Great, and singing the questions on everyone's minds. Their album is very post-Guantanamo, very now. You must see what they are doing.

Seeing Roky Erickson made me think he should've been playing at Kingston Mines. Blues choogle done choogled. Boredoms only had a forty-minute set, so they played two songs—phenomenal. I was totally high from eating a whole funnel cake and covered in powdered sugar. The guy from High on Fire was missing a tooth, shirtless, biker-y, and had his entire side covered in a half-finished rabid wolf head tattoo. All the girls I was with professed that he was their new crush. "I saw a picture of him once, passed out, holding his dick. He's from Oakland," said one. A dude missing a tooth is a dude that will give you an adventure.

They were so loud we all had to lie out on the grass under a faraway tree and eat more snacks swiped from catering, chew lemonade straws, ponder passing asses, outfits, tattoos, the drunkenness of hip frauds, and why no girls are in bands anymore. It was a fine time.

June 24, 2006

EXTRALIFE

Saturday was the Hold Steady video. It is a good thing not all one hundred people showed up because we had room for about thirty-three total. People later said they did not show because filming video is waiting around for twenty hours to act fake-excited in one-minute spurts. Which might be true when you are on the set of Sum 41's "Spooge Patrol" shoot, but this is the Hold Steady; they are a punk band on a punk budge, no time to spare. I got paid with a latte and a vegan muffin. It was like a Hold Steady show, except it lasted three hours, and they played the same song eight times all the way through. In between, the extras and the band just knocked back beers and ate nuts from a can. They played, and the first couple of times we faced one way on the set, then they played again and we faced the other way. It was not complicated and our enthusiasm was not fake. Miles and I got assigned to stand right in front of Craig the whole time, and so we were flecked with his spit.

Other highlights: Miles punched the air on the drum fill and lost his glasses on the floor. I held Craig's

BlackBerry for him during the shoot, and I sent horribly sappy emails to the rest of the band from his email account, detailing, in florid language, just how special I thought our relationship was and how much I thought being in a band with them was a fun experience.

Late night: I saw Miles play an acoustic show, and it was great. His lyrics got stuck in my brain, and I was singing them all day on the bike. Just refrains. Miles has songs that have lines about last call at Rainbo that drop bon mots like "And we all lie / for / a little / heeeaaaad." The people who played after him were a stark contrast. The next performer had a keyboard-piano and if I had to guess I would say his musical influence is the Capitol Steps. Lyrically, it was more like . . . Rufus Wainwright as a fourteen-year-old chess champion. Oh, and he was dressed in pleat fronts, dirty white Reeboks, a too-small women's argyle sweater vest. When he would sing "Baby" it was like . . . a formatting error. If that dude with the piano has ever called anyone "baby" in real life, other than an actual newborn, I would be shocked.

And somehow, the next dude managed to be more wrongly fangled than the Virgin Caddy. He started out with this delicate but dramatic Skip Spence/Belle and Sebastian sound. I thought I might be able to hang, but then came the chorus of his first song. He was trailing in and out with his voice, which was going from whispery to bedroom quiet to leaves-twinkling-in-the-breeze loud. And then he sang, "We get lost / . . . on Lonely Street / We lose our . . . irection." And then he repeats what sounds like "we lose our erection" four times. I had to kick Miles to keep from falling out of my plastic lawn chair and giggling in juvenile hysterics.

October 09, 2005

I WAS PLAYING IN A DROP D PUNK BAND/
WE CALLED SEAQUEST

Went out to see Har Mar Superstar, the solo project
of the drummer of my high school band. He played
to a packed house of horny, horny women baring
summer-celebratory cleavage and bemused dudes. I
stood between a superfan who was elated when Sean
gave her a rabid bit of mouth-to-mouth during the
Karen-O parts of the single, and a club of naughty
secretaries who were jealous of the kiss. They asked
the girl for a report seconds after Sean's tongue left
her mouth. The secretaries may actually be executives
for all I know—I am only going by their low-heeled
pumps. They were boobzillas all, and made a grind
train among the six of them. They pawed Sean's crotch
whenever he would get near enough. Sean's new trick
was lowering his pants and exposing his pubic hair,
plucking out a fingerful and *SPRINKLING HIS
PUBES ON THE FRONT ROW LIKE PIXIE
DUST*. That made all the women go nuts unlike anything I have seen at a show previously. I nearly peed
myself laughing.

April 05, 2005

THE GHOST OF YOU LINGERS

I should have taken a picture, but my words will have to suffice. I showed up to interview Annie Clark and she was dressed like a haute couture vato. Some Japanese bizarrity grey-plaid high-button shirt, white billowy tank underneath, high black jeans, white witch shoes. We talked quietly in the theater manager's office. The manager's assistant came back while we were talking, to use his computer, and we said we'd be done shortly, it was just a quickie. He told us there have been a lot of quickies in this office. It struck us speechless, and then he just started reeling it back in. Not speaking from experience. Not recently. He's only heard. Not like, heard, but heard about it. He's never seen it. I looked at Annie—we had been displaced off of the office chairs that the man needed back and were in the corner doing the yard squat—and said, "You know, actually, I think we got enough. We're done. Thanks."

I left to go eat with Matt, New Tokyo was a wait, so we gambled on a place and gambled wrong. S'was gross. We got back to the theater and sat down with enough time to speculate about what kind of people like John Vanderslice. The people in front and in back of us, older daters; others, proactively tweemo. But next to us, boy-girl braces-faces on a giddy date. Then five drunk douches filled out the rest of our row. When Annie came on stage in her wrinkly school uniform via Balenciaga hot-ensemb, the show-talkers, who were obviously "in their cups" as they used to say, were yakking loud like they were trying to be heard over the sound of the Green Line train pulling into the station. One of the guys yelled in Borat-voice "I Like!," and someone else wolf-whistled. Annie did not blink, she just pile-drove some din and some fancy-free hammer-on into our faces.

April 14, 2007

SICK CRATIN' 'TIL DAWN

The DJ booth was built for the Euro-trained and those who can manage three tables and a mixer like a 747 steering console. Miles is beside me helping me dig the crate, filling my requests for "water, light on the ice" in exchange for the drink tickets I never use anyway. He is my copilot, watching the road, so I can check the map: "The girl gang is dancing now, you should go with the Technotronic or Jay Z." Or after I went with M.O.P, "Oh . . . oh! Yep, I think you lost them . . . well, fuck 'em!" As he reaches over me and turns up the gain, throwing his hands up, we're hollering along, "Your life or your jewels?!" to the empty dance floor.

I forgot, until Miles flyered me, that Binocular (#2 in the streets!) is appearing in our usual uphill holiday weekend slot at the Bottle this week. You missed us the day after Halloween, the day after Thxgvg, the day after motherfunking Xmas, and now, now, NOW! Here is a chance to enjoy the ass end of Holy Week with us. That's right, A Very Special Binoculars Easter, this Sunday at the Empty Bottle. Miles is threatening to dress as Jesus. I will be spining direct from a basket filled with shredded plastic grass. Hot times. Hot times! Three cute girls we flyered swore they would show up, get drunk, and dance. There is your incentive!

March 24, 2005

CAREER OPP

First off, before it was time to talk to the eager froshes of DePaul University about "women in ze music biz," I inexplicably drank two cups of coffee, the first caffeine I have had in two years. I stuck by my mantra of "no fighting with audience or fellow panelists," but I think I sounded like I had just done a thirty-foot rail of speed.

Secondly, teenagers are genius. They are awkward and have no time for any adult's bullshit. They offered elaborate theories on the Omaha scene myth and had an active interest in debunking Conor Oberst's talent in the daylight. "Why is *SPIN* so on his dick? Why do they keep saying he is the greatest songwriter of my generation? He's not! Everything I read is like, 'He's Bob Dylan! He's drunk!' Give me some insight that will make me care!" said the sophomore sage. I was like, "Totes. Totes."

They asked me why thirty-year-old musician dudes are always dating their friends who are nineteen and stupid, and does that creep me out like that creeps them out. (Yes. It does.) They asked me if all guys in bands are like that. I said, some, but it has more to do with being a thirty-year-old dude in an emo band, I think.

They told me about being treated like groupies in every internship they have had, and asked me what they can do so that the men they work for stop flirting with them and take them seriously. I did not know where to start with that one. They told me about how when they are booking a show, the promoter calls them *honey*, and how do they deal with it, without pissing him off, 'cause they need to get bands into that venue. They told me stories I lived a decade ago, and it was depressing. They gave me all the brownies I could eat, firm handshakes, too, and then I headed home. Huzzah to the ladies of DePaul Career Fest 2005 and their fighting spirit.

March 10, 2005

BECAUSE THE NIGHT BELONGS TO LARGE PROFESSOR, BECAUSE THE NIGHT BELONGS TO US!

The dance floor is actually just some stairs. I danced with Hunter and Vanessa. I told Hunter his outfit made him look like early '80s David Crosby: white seersucker suit, sleeveless tie-dye shirt, a serious beard, some gold chains, and a rope belt. "Awesome, thanks." Inexplicably, he was yelling, "E-BAY!" like one might yell, "Westsiiide!" during the breaks of songs, and then whiffing hits of VCR head cleaner from a little bottle. I asked him if inhalants are his drug of choice. He stopped dancing and thought about it seriously. "Yes, yes they are," he said, and started again.

Some guy with a camera was trying to take pictures and was in our dance zone. Hunter and I sand-wiched him aggressively, and Hunter, now down to the sleeveless shirt, did a move which can only be described as "giving him the armpit." Once the guy relented, Hunter said, "Cameras are just so . . . stupid," paused, puts his hands to his head, kind of sat in an invisible chair, quickly stood back up, raised his hands in the air, and screamed, "WHOA!," then went back to dancing.

Then El-P ceded the decks to Peanut Butter Wolf after a decent string of old-school surefire. El-P's skill with the mixer left a little to be desired; his touch with the fader could adequately be described as "violent." Upon exiting the booth, he stood with Kathryn and me and mocked his own lack of technique. His humility was refreshing. He played Public Enemy five times in an hour, which was admirable as well.

Mr. Butter Wolf then made two turntables seem like four; he was cutting and mixing with the deft finesse for which he is known. Slick Rick into "Walk on the Wild Side" into "I Shot The Sheriff" into "Deee-Lite Theme" into "It Takes Two" into "Message to You Rudy" into "The Tide Is High" into EPMD. If you ask me to tell you my fantasy, it is something like that.

Then El-P was back on and he played some shit from back when all rap songs were eight or eleven minutes long, then, after realizing that was a fatal move, threw on Large Professor. He was having fun, and that's really what matters.

Meanwhile, I spent this time standing by the bar, waiting for my water with ice and a straw, talking about my new haircut with acquaintances amid fancy Puma shoes in saturated matte colors that were arranged between the Baileys and the Icy Hot bottles at this store opening party.

I ate my ice and called it a night.

November 13, 2004

Chicago

SPEND A NIGHT OR TWENTY WITH
PETER WOLF

Oh, strange day to love and hate. Mid of it, I rang JR. Turned out he was a block up the street, eating a pear in front of the library, waiting for his turn at the computers. He has to stay on top of his fantasy league. I showed up stomping, hot with the new news from my landlord—turns out our lease is seven months long, not a year. And if we wanna stay, we gotta come up with $300 more a month, and he knows we can't. He knocked on the door to say he's showing the apartment tomorrow, purely rhetorically, and P.S. here's two months' notice. Post-library, we wandered with half an aim, and jinxed saying, "I'll watch anything with Lee Marvin in it!"

Talked briefly of the strangeness of being in the world. Ran into Nora and went to the dollar store: pencils for her, a notebook for JR, nothing for me. Store soundtrack: pan-fluted version of "I Am a Rock." After an errand to pick up JR's mashed potatoes and gravy, after quizzical discussion about the concepts and practice of a "career," after much hoofing, but before edits, we toured the very tidy apartment house of an old woman who had linoleum floors and three canaries. She was reading Anne Rice en español.

This early morning, while I sat on the bench outside Daley Center, tourists in fake train cars helmed by bullhorned guides pulled up. Everyone snapped shots of the grand Picasso, staying far enough away to avoid being accosted by pigeons or hurried attorneys or wafts of acrid piss baked into the sidewalk. Who wants a picture of the fucking Daley Center from a block away, even with the statue? Where must you come from for that to be picture-worthy?

To love this city, I attest, you must also hate it dispassionately.

June 13, 2006

First all-day bike excursion of the year. It feels like one hundred years, condensed into five hours, à la *Raintree County*. I went to the car wash to get quarters and dudes were playing Frankie Beverly super loud. Then I took the quarters to the gas station to pump up my bike tire. There was a solitary dude there polishing his rims to ultra-loud Frankie Beverly as well. Post-pump, I aimed towards United Center. The empty mega-block where they tore down the housing projects is slated to become a massive condo development, according to a new sign; not sure if it's yuppie or CHA development. I wonder what it will be like when that block goes from empty to two hundred bedrooms.

I turned the wrong way down a street and had to ride on the sidewalk; there was a grip of ladies in hats leaving First Baptist to slalom around.

I turned down Washington and two or three blocks below Ashland, I heard a drum corps banging away. I turned the corner to see what was going on and it was a uniformed junior high marching band loitering against a wall. Banging, tooting, sharing ear buds.

Dreams do come true.

I got to the corner and stared at them a little, wondering why they were there, and when I turned to look in the opposite direction, all I could see for blocks were blue-and-white floats, other marching bands, and roughly five hundred kiddos in traditional Greek outfits: pom-pom shoes, tunics, embroidered vests. It was the Hellenic pride parade (my guess), and every Greek Orthodox school, parish, club, bank, and sundry community organization was out in special getups, milling around, waiting for the parade to start so they could get up on their floats. The traffic cop told me it started in an hour. I had time to get to the library and back and still see it. I got to the Harold Washington branch and hustled back as fast as I could. I wound up seeing the whole parade! Best part: a reenactment society that had to do with 1921 Greece, clad in super-tight black outfits with bullet belts; they looked like they were in From Ashes Rise.

I biked from there through the meatpacking district, past Mr. City and Bee Jay Meat Market, then past the ADM mill, past a pile of curious CDs (Connells, Poi Dog Pondering) in a tunnel. On Milwaukee, headed towards the Crotch, I saw a dude eat shit on his bike and almost get mushed by a black Mercedes. He was ok. I gagged hard when he showed me his wound, which looked like a banana peel slit open with banana squishin' out, had already bruised blue, and had gravel in it.

The Crotch was mayhem. Shirtless Wrigleyville bros in wraparound Oakleys yelling like they owned the world; frost 'n' tip ladies and dudes in major vehicles were out in surplus numbers. Also, an unnamed emo celebrity driving a black H3. Exiting the Walgreens, a young lady with a skaterbangs mohawk walked past me and smiled a huge giddy smile. Her shirt read "I FUCKED YOUR BOYFRIEND" in Olde English lettering. Sometimes I feel like the world is coarsening faster than I can handle.

Then! I saw JR on the street and we agreed to stencil Bayard Rustin T-shirts later on. Then, on the wee median, I saw the kid who played the organ all summer long. He was back out, now with an accordion. I requested "Moon River" and he said he didn't know how to play any songs at all. He was just out on the corner making people happy with the accordion. It's his mission, since he got arrested for playing the organ. He told me he's really doing it because, "Obviously, this is the last summer that Wicker Park is going to really be Wicker Park, because, well, Filter is leaving." Apparently the loss of a *Reality Bites*–grade cafe will really seal the gentrification deal for him. Up until that point, I was thinking I should do a story on his tender all-summer accordion initiative. His nostalgia for the "Wicker Park of two years ago" was enough to turn my stomach. (Has Wicker Park even been Wicker Park since Algren left in '75? Since they stopped finding bodies in the alleys, circa 1999? Boo-fucking-hoo, the "cool" shopping area is not very cool anymore!)

I sped off towards ice cream, towards home. When I got home the neighborhood kids were on the corner unison-yelling "Honk! . . . Honk! . . . Honk!" Duetting along with a car alarm.

March 25, 2007

AMERICAN CITY, I LOVE YOU TOO

Since enacting my Lenten pact to only drive for work-related errands, I am experiencing Chicago's deep mantic powers on the daily. This is not to say I did not love this hobbled city, potholed and blue-collared, from the moment I arrived six years and three days ago. But just that having to bike, sometimes too far, to new and inconvenient places, and often on the same old route down Damen, I might as well be seeing it for the first time. All the apartments illuminated with the blue glow of a TV, the living room walls gridlocked by mounted collector plates, scrubbed-clean dudes in light-rinse jeans drinking beer from a can on a leather couch (viewed so easily due to the two-story basement-to-ceiling windows in the front of their new construction condos). The patinaed crosses and gilded domes of all the bright Ukrainian churches. A dude in a red convertible Ferrari, with a vanity plate reading FERRARI, holding his dick while he cruises.

Just stuff you miss when you're in the car with B96 up too loud.

On Saturday Al—and Nora, the chain-smoking young sweetness he hangs with—and I biked 14.4 miles to the psychedelic art show over at Texas Ballroom in Pilsen. On the way, Nora and I chattered in the bike lane about girl stuff (Lacan). On the way back, Nora lollygagged behind and I took off ahead, seeing just how fast I could go on a friend's fancy track bike. I was re-enacting scenes from *Breaking Away* on the barren byways in the heart of Cook County at 2 a.m. on a spring Sunday.

Taking Damen Avenue from one side of town to another, you get a good span of Chicago, something practical to counter the highlights reel of Lake Shore Drive. Damen is all that is old, burnished, and lopsided. It is profoundly comforting to live in a city that doesn't give a shit and loves you how you are, because it is every bit as marred, bereft, and cocky as you are.

We came through Pilsen's strip malls, past the 24/7 donut diner, over the freeway overpass where all the trucks exit for the mills and factories, through Latino revitalization and SAIC students tangling up on 18th, through nine straight blocks of taquerias and

storefront churches, past bondo'd Cutlasses spring-
ing tinny *umpa-umpa* bandas, then through the five
blocks of the tunnel underneath the train land bridge
that is strangely clean because it's so vast and sketchy
that no one walks through it (not even to tag it),
which empties out to broken cement parking lots and
sprawling brick warehouses that once served industries
that no longer exist, past public housing bungalows
isolated from their now-demolished twin—the Ida
B. Wells Homes in Bronzeville—past Little Italy's
ass-end, through the hospital campus with its wide,
presidential-appellative streets of Roosevelt and Washington—its spartan gutters—into the direct arterials
to downtown, over the bridge that spans I-290,
through a Near West Side neighborhood holding out
against gentrification, past the parking lots of the
United Center—trashed after the Bulls vs. Golden
State Warriors game hours earlier, past the long swath
of empty lots and boarded up CHA low-rises, tiny
mountains of debris and weedy knolls on either side
of the Green Line train elevated tracks—the parts of
West Madison St. that have never been rebuilt since
being burned in the riots—then underneath the tracks
where the best car chase in the Blues Brothers movie

takes place, past two women singing a Mary J. Blige song together on the corner, past a gaggle of hipster friends of friends in funny outfits waving and hugging while exiting a square dance at Open End, past the Drag City office, underneath my favorite train bridge, then three more blocks, where I hung a right on Ohio and rode no-handed the last two blocks to my little house.

March 03, 2004

BALLAD OF DRE AND JAMMIES GIRL

There is a house of trouble down at the end of the block. I am pretty sure there are some sales going on thereabouts, though sometimes it's just boys with their shirts off, swearing. One of them is this kid, Dre. He's about 4'11", just past teenaged, scrawny, and white. I assume his name is Dre because that's what it says on his face—in cursive, ear to jaw, a jagged poke tat in lieu of a sideburn. He hardly has any work on his arms, it's like 80 percent above the shoulders. He hangs out next to the car wash drinking Big Gulps. Anyhow, Dre is currently associating with a girl with stringy blonde hair who wears pajama pants out of the house. They argue often and loudly and at some point he always walks away and just keeps walking. And she follows, trailing twenty to thirty feet behind, haranguing him. He will walk all around the neighborhood, never able to shake her, and she never quite catches up. I imagine that everyone within a two-block radius of here knows their business. They are on their second trip around the block now, and she is still calling him a pussy asshole for fighting with her in front of her own mother. The first time by, he was hollering about what a fucking bitch she is, but now he's solemnly speedwalking, punctuating her harangues with worn calls of "UUUGHHHHH!" He should really look into getting a bike or something.

June 30, 2007

SUMMA

Yesterday at dusk teenage neighborhood boys fought hard under the tree, breaking car windows out with the force of each other's bodies.

Cops came quick. Two boys went over a fence and down an alley, two boys stood dripping blood in the driveway.

Now pyramided piles of Pontiac Safe-T-Glass are in the street; you gotta ride around 'em.

June 12, 2007

WAR, WHIMSY & HORRORS

A woman with a smoky voice is standing three stories below my living room window yelling "RICKY!" over and over with long pauses between. Her tone does not distinguish whether Ricky is a man or a dog. We have fifteen windows in the apartment and most of them are open now. Matt theorized that maybe once the trees grow back their leaves, it'll be quieter—tree insulation. Maybe the ruffling of the leaves will be a white noise that'll block out old yellers.

Ricky!

Rick-eee!

March 26, 2007

HOLY ROLL HER

Tonight, after I refused a "Do You Want To Spend Eternity in HEAVEN or HELL?!" tract from some Jehovah-bent folks outside the downtown library, a kid followed me down the block with copies of the pamphlets in hand, swearing at me for not taking them. At first I was like, Am I imagining this? No—there was an eleven-year-old walking five steps behind me muttering, "Whuddup, bitch? Why didn't you take a pamphlet? You can just ignore him like that? Huh? *Beeitch!*" I finally stopped and turned to look at him. I asked him, "Excuse me?"—like, curious—and he got loud, looked me up and down.

"Yes, excuse you, bitch! What, you don't want one of these? You don't need one? Think you can just keep walking?" He moved right up next to me. He was not even up to my shoulders, and I am 5'3".

I had no idea where to begin to address what was going on. Like, is the kid going to fight me, or should I explain that I did not take a heaven/hell pamphlet because, despite actively celebrating Holy Week, I am more a Jesus-y jouisseur than trad Christian, per se, and do not believe in the binary ideal of heaven/hell as something we experience in death, but rather something experienced as we live, and so I do not need the pamphlet? I mean, I think the kid could have understood the jagged dichotomy of my personal theology; he was, after all, a child evangelist addressing an adult stranger as "bitch." Before I could say anything at all he snickered at me and said "Bitch!" once again for good measure, and then, mysteriously, turned and walked into a shoe store that only sells women's high heels.

March 17, 2005

SANDBURG'S PART

Looking at this picture of Carl Sandburg on the cover of *Time* from decades past, it's difficult to imagine a time, an era, in this or the previous American century in which a poet could be on the cover of a magazine. It's a strange thought. Look at that wonderful eye of his. A person with a walleye is never on the cover of anything anymore; it's a shame. The left eye is accusing, the right one believes in the good of man and loves you from the start.

Carl Sandburg had the same exact haircut from the time he was old enough to have a haircut until the time he was dead.

Carl Sandburg was invoked a bit last year because he came to Sufjan in a dream, in a dream in a song that many people liked, and asked, "Are you writing from the heart?" Maybe spectral-Sandburg was being protective, custodial, wanting to determine whether Sufjan, as a muse, was worthy of the city. Seems like a believable line of questioning for him.

In the introduction to *Harvest Poems 1910–1960*, Mark Van Doren says Sandburg can be boiled down to these final lines of "Grass": *What place is this? / Where are we now?* Tuff rhetoricals seem to be his forte.

I'm still just getting familiar, fifty-seven pages in, but the getting is easy.

From "Gone:"
So we all love a wild girl keeping a hold
On a dream she wants

There is an entire summer in those lines!

May 28, 2006

REPPING HARD FOR THE LOCAL

As if that *Vice* guide for the Intonation Festival wasn't bad enough (written by someone who hasn't lived here in three years), the new *SPIN* has a guide to Chicago that if anyone abided by, save for the recommended stop at Reckless, they would believe Chicago was (only! merely!) a clean place inhabited by soused whiteys. I think whoever wrote it actually hates Chicago. I mean, why else would anyone with a modicum of Chicago pride send an out-of-towner to the Pontiac for a good time? I mean, sure, if that person is a beefy, shirtless dude looking to show off his tribal tats and nipple peircings to hungover Jeep chicks who are turned on by that sort of thing—yes, *by all means.* C'mon, there are at least eighty other bars in the area where you can work on your base tan and drink off last night's bender. Also, why recommend Underdog as one of the best five places in town to eat?! Everyone knows that for special dogs you go to Hot Doug's, and that you go to Underdog to see a dude in a white hat drop trou and press his nuts to the window glass to cheer up his date, who has just vomited last call into the street. Also, why would anyone recommend a stop at the Apple store—and not, like Rainforest Cafe, or *geez*, a fucking Target for that matter? Fuck landmarks, the Sox, nice views or the 150-odd museums—VISIT *STORES*!

July 18, 2006

THE TYRANNY OF DISTANCE VS. POWER OF PROXIMITY

I did a dumb thing last night, something I knew better about and managed to stave off doing for the last seven weeks of living in LA. I looked at pictures of my friends and life back home. I wondered when I will go home. I've been avoiding that question. But once I looked at the pictures, there was not a thing I didn't miss. Marcus Garvey Burgers from Soul Veg. Animals. My bike. All my deeply weird and funny and stinky friends. Books I had checked out from the library and was in the middle of. Intersections. All the bike punks with U-lock outlines worn into their back pockets. How fucking loud it is all the time. I miss how when you walk down the street in Chicago, you are expected to say hello to people and if they have a dog, say "hi puppy," compliment their dog or ask its name (at least!). On the park trail here in LA, people react to that question as if I'd just asked if they birthed their dog vaginally.

June 22, 2008

MISSED CONNECTIONS

I saw you last night and haven't been able to stop thinking about you since. It was super crowded, I know you did not see me, but I was immediately smitten and could not stop staring, even though to get a glimpse I had to look through another girl's ponytail. Would love to see you again sometime soon, maybe someplace less crowded?
Me: Jessica Hopper
You: Doug Gillard's Ripping Guitar Solos

My female friend and I were sitting in the corner booth at Sweet Maggie B's, and you came in with your two friends as the girls at the register were closing and began making comments about how the pie was probably a week old. But you kept looking over at us when you said these things and kept trying to engage us in conversation; you obviously wanted to talk. I bumped into you on the way out and did not bother saying sorry.
Me: Annoyed woman dressed like Paddington bear
You: Old white dude in a leather bomber coat from a

car dealership, shitfaced drunk at 9 p.m. on a Friday, looking to harass every girl in sight

I was in the third row, standing with friend, sandwiched around a bunch of talkers on dates, off-time foot tappers, and women with pokey purses—still nothing could distract me from you. I have seen you at Schubas before, but you look different without the beard. It made me notice you in a way I never have before. You had my rapt attention. I hope you do not think this is creepy!
Me: Jessica Hopper
You: Richard Buckner's teeth

February 04, 2006

NOTES

I picked up a copy of Patti Smith's *Babel* at Myopic, this aft, for a loose $10.50. The name of the previous owner was on the first page, in delicate script: "Edith Frost."

In a yard down the street, someone has up a mono-lithic inflatable snowmen ensemble: a dad snowman flanked by two half-pint snowmen lit from within. The little snow dude on the left has a defect, one would guess, and is now half-deflated and bobbing forward, carrot nose folding up as he bumps face-first into the larger snowman's snowy crotch-zone. The mittened hand of the larger snowman is affixed to the back of little snowdude's head. This slowly deflat-ing, lewd snowman scene is in the front yard of one of those new-construction condos with the two-story liv-ing room windows; how are the owners not noticing this ménage? Perhaps they are facedown and drooling Corona-spittle onto their white leather couches. Per-haps they are subversive pervs who rigged the whole thing up themselves. Perhaps.

December 23, 2005

WHATCHOOKNOWABOUTTHAT?!

I've been telling people, "I've been busy, working at the library a lot," and they assume that I've gotten a job there. I had to change locales, as the two-month-long reroofing that's going on above me doesn't give a fuck about my manuscript due date. So. I ride the same route, stay for the same time, pack my 'puter, books, and snacks, settle in, and give myself permission to move to another room if someone starts making noise. Or if the guy that sorta lives in the library sidles up nearby. He mutters "shitmotherfuckshiiiiyatcocksuckerfuckinshiiiyat" nonstop in a low bass voice that rumbles through earplugs. Part of the appeal of the library is being in silence with a bunch of people, all furiously ploughing books, but not everyone abides by that, which is the other part of the library's appeal. The library belongs to everyone.

It is finals week and the reading room is packed with collegiate refugees. Yesterday a ponytailed girl sat down across from me and pushed up the sleeves of her ASU hoodie and suddenly filled the room with the unmistakable sillage of Bath & Body Works Cherry

Blossom Splash body spray, which brought on flash-backs of every strip club I've ever been to. I moved to the hall so as not to barf, where the security guard promptly busted me for eating a banana. (I have a neutral fascination with him. He's got a flat face and weak chin, and his Cupid's bow is so arched that he looks like he's sneering and smelling hot trash at the same time; it lends an air of menace as he makes the rounds, chastising the homeless dudes for sleeping and teens snarfing Cheetos. I think he takes a lot of pride in his job, he looks really satisfied pushing in stray chairs. He is very thin and his uniform is much too big for him in a way that reminds me of when I used to make Kleenex outfits for my paper dolls.) From nowhere he appeared and squatted down so as to make eye contact with me: "Go ahead and finish your banana, but you can't eat in the library. It's cool if you wanna drink water, that's the policy, but when there's food in the library, the librarians get shit and I catch heat too." Classic good cop with a cuss thrown in so I don't think he's "the Man." He's just a guy doing his job, and his job is sneaking up on people and their bananas.

April 30, 2008

THIS PARTICULAR HEAT

The score upon returning home: plants *dead*, cats *alive*.

A trio of friends surprised me at baggage claim, they crept up behind me, and I turned around wondering, what's that smell? It was Miles's moustache!

Back home, I went on a long walk with JR and then another with Ben. Big loops to get tacos and back both times. Same tacos for different people from the same place, many hours apart. Picante at 1:42 a.m. was all slobbery and slack-faced men of the office, nighted-out and ousted by last call, dress shirts untucked over breakless casual pants. Their voices were loud and their jokes were louder and their walk was a sideways amble, like that of a cartoon animal that's been hit in the head. On the curb, some white hats and a date-night woman argued, "I can too, I did know that song was Radiohead. I LOOOVE RADIOHEAD!"

The teasing boy replied only, "I'M GETTING A CIGARETTE."

She yelled back, "I WANT A CIGARETTE, TOO. I DID TOO KNOW IT WAS RADIOHEAD!" They were standing five feet apart, I was lamping on a planter between them; I believed her, she was emphatic. Those boys were just ragging on her.

In Chicago, you are invisible to these people unless you are DJing or they are really wasted. You are a ghost unless you are part of their crew, or at least their caste. The more drunk they become, the more they are aware of us scuffed-up old kids. When they see you, they need to know, as if baffled by their sudden discovery: Why are you eating your tacos over the trash can?

Living in a city of drunk jocks will keep you punk forever.

In LA, what can you rebel against—the sprawl of humanity? The zombie Pat O'Brien in the Coachella VIP? White smog skies? Desire?

I missed this boisterous, insular, tiny-big city. Everything is smaller than I remembered. I feared I would

come home and feel dislodged and adrift, but I don't.
I feel home.

December 23, 2005

NATURAL'S NOT IN IT

When you go outside in LA, it is like walking into the smoking car on Amtrak, although you'd have to have taken a long train ride in the previous few decades to remember that relic. Or perhaps more like whatever room your grandpa smoked Winstons and watched reruns in, except the air is not rich with the high-notes hair tonic. Here it hits the eyes just before the lungs. It is not campfire, it is smoldering plastic siding and melting porch railing and dresses and trashcans and truck tires. During the day the sky is milky and thick and at night it's hard pink striae and dark-too-soon.

How do Californians manage these disasters that you cannot prevent or predict and can barely fight? In the Midwest, we have shovels. We know when tornadoes are coming. The naturalness of these LA disasters is foreign to me.

November 16, 2008

SHOW ME A CAT TOY AND I WILL SHOW YOU THE WORLD COME ALIVE

The train time 'tween home and "the shithole formerly known as St. Louis™" is besting itself every week. Heading down Thursday was pedestrian—I shared a seat with a woman engrossed in a bodice-ripper paperback that must have been salacious because every time I would so much as turn my head towards her she'd shift the book away. I was just trying to see over her to the kid doing his Photoshop retouching homework on his laptop, diligently attempting to follow the 72 pt. Helvetica instructions typed over the unkindly lit portrait of a woman: "smooth chin, whiten teeth." He did, eventually making her way-back teeth gleam incandescently. Her chin looked like Richard Dreyfuss's mashed potato mountain from *Close Encounters* once he finished with it.

This time, rather unmercifully, there was a mass of people who brought nothing to do on the five-and-a-half-hour ride except tend their flip phones and Sidekicks. The woman next to me called no fewer than sixteen people, and after each would give me a synopsis:

"He's going to call me back" or "No one was home." Later, after a half-dozen abortive attempts to change her outgoing message (my favorite: "All y'all leave your message," which she scrapped) I offered her my library book, which I hadn't read, but she had. She gave me a synopsis of the first few chapters with the sort of breathless recounting one saves for gossip; I wasn't expecting *Coast of Chicago* to be so dishy, but now I am doubly excited.

While we had been in the ticket line, another passenger had tried rather valiantly to pick her up. He had a deep orange tan and smelled hungover. For the duration of the ride, he cruised her, hit her with blunt compliments for which there was no rejoinder, and made promises of a shared sippy cup of Bud Lite up in the bar car. He had no game, and by the Lincoln stop was resorting to high-fives upon his return from the bathroom, a presumptive and gross burden to put on a friend, let alone a stranger, after you have just drunkenly pissed in a tiny, filthy, jolting room distinguishable from an open sewer only by its display of a stainless steel "mirror" and a little sign prohibiting you from flushing needles and diapers.

February 23, 2009

R U THAT SOMEBODY?

It is south hot and the town is a ghost town, due to heat or holiday. I have been alone on the street for blocks. Being unwittingly, cripplingly high on cold medicine makes my bike ride feel like a screw tape, one mile per hour against the wind with no breath to breathe on. Dog barks reverberate off buildings, cars whir and whinny, bass drops doppler from passing cars. Its all-together menace is pure *Psychic Powerless*. Neighbor babies pram Pampers-only and all the old dudes porch it in their undershirts watching all the young dudes yell into cell phones, chains popping against their sternums in time with their gait, everyone sweating the same.

July 01, 2006

ALL THINGS GO/ALL THINGS GO

Today is the twenty-fifth anniversary of Nelson Algren's death. I feel like *Chicago: City on the Make* is representative of the city-soul, with its do-right whores and Division Street devils and ghosts at last call, old-world Poles mopping the sidewalk with someone's face, most everyone living at the fringes—more, still, this city than Sandburg's "hogbutcher to the world." Didion says there is a whole novel in one line of Henry James's. I think the same of Algren. All that misery under the streetlight halos, real people misfortune, drunk boxers in love with good-luck girls, "Ogden Avenue eyes."

Walked down Chicago Ave. this morning with JR on our near-daily constitutional, me looking like an overgrown boy scout, JR looking like a king hell brawler with his shiner, stitches ringed 'round his eye, and sleeveless, bootleg Mötley Crüe shirt. The streets are mean, but we look even meaner.

May 09, 2006

CAVALRY OF LIGHT

The boys I hang out with, all of them, are not feeling my shoes. Miles says they are "total mom" and Matt asked me if they are "even supposed to be cute." Today, JR and I saw a lady on the bus, and she was rocking my exact same look, down to the shoes. She was about seventy-five. I am wildly orthopedic and I am not going back. Confident women of a certain age can kick shit however they like, wild-styled, and thus I am only SAS nurse lifts in taupe, wooden shoes, and dollar store flip-flops from here on out.

Other than this, little to report. Puttering, errands, pep talk, falling in love with old people on the bus.

Yesterday was so lovely all I could think of was that Sufjan song "Casimir Pulaski Day," which is about gratitude and the death of a pretty girl. I was thinking mostly of that line "What the lord has made." I got flowers for Valentine's Day for the first time in my life, I bought delicious DayGlo treats at the Tahoora Bakery on Devon, I rode my bike in the sun and forty-six-degree weather.

I am seven kinds of in love with Chicago, a love so powerful it blots out everything else.

February 15, 2006

BLOCKAPELLA FREESTYLE

Took Wood to whatever street the United Center is
on.

CHA projects are still coming down slow: bent girders
hang building bits outta burnt-up bedrooms painted
institutional peach and tan on the nineteenth floor,
a wrecking ball suspended and still beside a halved
superstructure. "New Development. New Neighborhood." So says the sign outside the temporary trailer
realty office. Pedaling the two-block bracket between
fallow glass lots that have stayed empty since '68 and
the unmarred blacktop of the United Center parking
lot, I think of what I know about these blocks: the
tiny chairs I dumpstered when they tore down the
school and the news anchor that got shanked in the
neck in the lot, and lived, and is now a motivational
circuit speaker. Here's to overcoming adversity, tiny
chairs, and the rolling blight of bright brick new construction condos, on blast.

May 22, 2005

HAVING ANSWERED SO I TURN ONCE MORE

Sandburg writes much about the new skyscrapers of Chicago being lifted, lifting the city, Chicago built and rebuilt, in "Windy City" and "Good Morning, America"—in those poems, they are valiant and triumphant. Their triumph is in the toil and labor as much as it's symbolic of progress and modernity. The night I got home, JR pointed out that the glowing tower that got bigger while I was gone, the thing I would fall asleep looking at every night since it came twinkling into view this early spring, is, in fact, the Trump Tower. Since then I have kept the right-side curtain of my room pulled on it. I liked it better when I thought it was a very tall parking structure or that twirling building that'll be the tallest in the world. The building having a name and identity changes my feelings about it; the toil of leather-handed men, and building something very tall, was progress in 1928, but now I think that continual triumph is a harbinger of ruin. But maybe it's just a building.

July 15, 2008

BACK TO THE BOOGIE

I could write about Los Angeles. I could tell you about the desert at night. I could tell you what it is like to hang out with people whom you thought for years you would see next at their funeral. But it's a story for another time.

I have been back in the Chi-Boogie since 1 a.m. Wednesday, and I have already taken a vow not to leave the Central Time Zone again for weeks, in trembling ode to—or rather, out of commitment to—Chicago and the Midwestern states, so sturdy and dirty and loving you back. The big lilac bushes in front of the house are blooming, almost obscuring all the supermarket circulars and take-out menus and metallic chip bags stuck in their branchy bottoms. The yard is a fantasia of schoolkid trash and perennials and weeds, with four shitty, rusted-up, and basketed Schwinns chained to the stoop as sentries.

I love Chicago as is, burnished perfect from years of disrepair. It makes me want to press my face to the rails of the Green Line L tracks and pledge allegiance to the long concrete meadows of Lake Street.

May 05, 2005

WEATHER REPORT

Discussing the weather is the domain of the all-the-way old, I know. I feel one hundred today, so it's par for the course. I will tell you this: I half-slept through an hour of NPR fundraising until they got to the part where they said, "And at O'Hare it's sixty-one degrees," and I was like, "Oh, oh! Time to get up." I practically levitated out of my bed. Sixty-one is a lot of degrees to have all at once. I think it finally melted all the ice in the pipes under the house, because the water is back to tasting like it comes from a chimney, not a faucet. I imagine the warmness means the mouse that has been occasionally shackin' in my cutlery drawer will take leave. Once I knew he was in there, I just let him have it, stopped using the drawer. As a child, I read a lot of books with mouse protagonists. I know he's just in there taking a nap in the soup spoon, using a match as a cane and a thimble as a cup. I am not about to put a trap down, get the mouse all shook, and have blood shed on my IKEA forks, you know?

March 26, 2004

SONGS IN HEAVEN

Al and Nora do not have a phone, so they stop by, which I like. It's old-timey and small town-y and makes me wistful for back when cell phones did not exist and you just had to show up places and hope for the best. They stopped by today to use my phone and tell me about the piano recital happening at Heaven tonight.

The recital was a dress-up thing, but I dressed in fatigues by accident. Liz kept calling me "Fidel." The reciters were wearing fancy outfits by a local art school designer. Kimi wore a sheer lace dress and men's underwear; another girl, who sang the "Lacrimosa" from Mozart's *Requiem,* was dressed as a sailor-baby and tugged on her navy collar as she trilled. Faten wore a pirate's coat that was velvet and had one trillion buttons, plus ruffled panties like a baby wears. She had a drawn-on eyeliner moustache that curled up at the ends. She had to unzip and remove her knee-high leather-heeled boots to play Grieg's Norwegian Concerto. Not to play favorites, but she killed it with the Grieg.

People in Chicago like to dress up. I think it helps them justify the cocaine (mere hunch). Many of the people at the recital looked like they were going to a party on a sailboat. In 1983. It was the same way they dressed the last time I saw them grinding ass-up, high as hell, on the dance floor to Franz Ferdinand at whatever stupid loft party we were at. Al, who grew up going to recitals because his mother was a concert violist, was disconcerted by the amount of nipple-bearing for such an event.

I was not nearly as disconcerted by the glorious fuck-me flair of the outfits on the piano bench as I was by the nineteen-year-old boy next to me who had a heart and banner tattoo with the word "MORRISSEY" in it. Loving the Smiths is one thing, but loving Morrissey is another thing entirely.

August 11, 2004

"SOMETIMES NOTHIN' IS A REAL COOL HAND"

The heat is protracting the days here. Open arms for the respite in the cool nights that liberate us. Hands sticky on bike handles and bass necks and cigarette filters. We just wait. You can't do much else.

Last night I wanted air conditioning and lobotomizing entertainment. Instead I got air conditioning and *Spider-Man 2*. I spent the last forty minutes of it wishing I had brought a magazine to read. I called Miles and Morgan, they had been dousing their coke Slurpees with whiskey, they were pink and wet-looking when I arrived. They did not want to move. I joined them in their torpor. Morgan showed us scars from her surgery, spoke at length on her cat's urinary tract infection, and made us watch *Cool Hand Luke*. She and Miles argued about whose turn it was to buy cigarettes. The sweat from the back of my legs adhered me to the couch. No one spoke. No one moved. If I had not gotten up when I did, I am certain I would have died there.

Today, the humidity was the killer. All the babies in my neighborhood are stripped to visors and diapers, slicking the arms of the women protectors with their stinkless baby sweat. The man with the Michoacán cart has his shirt open, baring a portrait on his chest of what might be a grey panther head or a map of Oahu or dress socks in a pile. Shirtless men will soon be drunk or fighting, as that is what the weather dictates.

July 22, 2004

LISTEN GIRL / I AIN'T SAYIN' YOU'RE HELPLESS

Here at Casa Hopper, we are celebrating Holy Week by taking the plastic off the windows and trying to pry them open. We discovered last week that the man at the hardware sold us the wrong kind of Seal 'N Peel caulking and that we have evidently sealed ourselves in with some permanence. We now spend warmer mornings working away at it with our sharpest knife, contemplating our own idiocy.

We are also celebrating Holy Week by listening to Prince all day every day since Saturday 11 a.m. CST. Yesterday there were about two hours from our favorite former Black Panther and Chicagoan, Chaka Khan, from her 1978 album *Chaka*, but as of 9:04 a.m. we were listening to Prince again, in love with the whole world, and hoping the neighbors love hearing "Little Red Corvette" on repeat this loud this early.

March 30, 2004

VIOLATION OF THE PURELY IMAGINARY

The best part of coming home is flying over the inky lake at night and suddenly you can see exactly where Chicago begins and ends by the vast gridlay of the amber street lights.

Amen.

Goodnight, you dazzle-diamond kiddos, and good night, all.

November 14, 2007

ACKNOWLEDGMENTS

I am grateful to Alice Merrill for her invaluable cataloguing and archiving of my work, and for the suggestion of this book. Thanks to Naomi Huffman for the initial assemblage and edit, and for being an astute guide throughout. Matt Clark's patience, encouragement, and steadfast partnership allowed me the time and space to bring this project to completion—thanks, babe.

Special thank you to Tim Kinsella and all at Featherproof, Casey Kittrell and all at the University of Texas Press, and my agent, Claudia Ballard at WME, for handling this book with such care and consideration.

I am also in the debt of my friends who appear throughout these stories, for both their kindness and companionship, then and still.

A portion of the proceeds from this book will benefit **Young Chicago Authors,** an organization that helps young people tell their own stories about life in this city.